Wicked LEWISTON

A Sinful Century

STEVEN D. BRANTING

THE
History
PRESS

Published by The History Press
Charleston, SC 29403
www.historypress.net

First published 2015

Manufactured in the United States

ISBN 978.1.46711.795.1

Library of Congress Control Number: 2015946488

Notice: The information in this book is true and complete to the best of our knowledge. It is offered without guarantee on the part of the author or The History Press. The author and The History Press disclaim all liability in connection with the use of this book.

For Shann, whose patient and unflagging support kept me going through four volumes of Lewiston's history.

For Marvin Yates, my late college buddy with whom, in my memories, I can still laugh.

CONTENTS

ACKNOWLEDGEMENTS

This volume owes its completion to the willing assistance of many individuals whom I wish to acknowledge here:

Brian Birdsell (Lewiston Police Department)
Garry Bush (Idaho History Tours)
Sharon Harris (Juliaetta-Kendrick Heritage Foundation)
Bud Hurd (Lewiston Police Department)
Jenaleigh Kiebert (Idaho State Archives)
Amy Olson (Mary Virginia Gifford Olson Collection)
Molly Pashley (Joan Gasser Ely Family Archives)
Jonathan Sheldan (Vancouver Island Integrated Major Crimes Unit)
Monty Spears (Lewiston Police Department, retired)
Virginia Thompson Leonard and Jill Nock (Twin River Genealogical Society)
Marion Tustanoff (British Columbia Archives)
Dr. Priscilla Wegars (University of Idaho, emeritus)
Mary E. White-Romero (Nez Perce County Historical Society)

To link the reader to additional content, parenthetical references are provided throughout this book to stories and photographs that appeared in earlier volumes of the Lewiston history collection, such as *Historic Firsts*, pages 34–36, and *Hidden History*, pages 80–86.

Monetary amounts are paired with reasonably equivalent current values, as in this example for 1894: $2,500 ($66,000).

Introduction

CROOKED PATHS AND DEVIOUS COURSES

*It's a wicked world, and when a clever man turns his brain to crime
it is the worst of all.*
—*Arthur Conan Doyle,* The Adventure of the Speckled Band

The expression "the good ol' days" is deceptive. Not all things are worth repeating; no amount of paint will cover some imperfections. In the hands of an author the likes of Agatha Christie, P.D. James or Colin Dexter, the unpleasant complications of mayhem, mischief and murder are intellectual exercises, whodunits to be unraveled. And then there are the Mickey Spillanes, whose claims to fame are the grit and grime, the guts and gore, the messiness of their stories. Wickedness in the real world is an unequal combination of both perspectives, and every new fact further complicates the quest for solutions.

No one truly studied the roots of crime until the middle of the eighteenth century, and even then only in the context of free will and its relationship to punishment. Crime was thought to be an innate tendency. Criminology owes its beginnings to Cesare Lombroso, whose best work dates from the end of the nineteenth century. Varying schools of thought developed, giving rise to a complex array of theories for why people commit criminal acts.

Those explanations did agree on two concepts: people react to how they are treated, and they fail to consider the consequences of their reactions. Most of the people whom you will meet in this book were no more demons than you or I. Time and unforeseen circumstance befall us all. It is the rare individual who steals just to steal, kills just to kill or is corrupted for the mere pleasure of gain. Adrift in a town of temptations like Lewiston, impulses often won out over rational thought. City council members brazenly sold prime lots along Snake River Avenue to themselves in April 1879. In January 1889, the council removed one of its own members for a reason not recorded in its minutes. Oscar Wilde once quipped, "The only way to get rid of a temptation is to yield to it."

The modern role of law enforcement can complicate our perspective of crime and the control of it in the past. The term "chief of police" was not officially used in Lewiston until March 1901, when the city amended its charter. Before that date, Lewiston had town marshals who were elected to terms of one year (*Historic Firsts* 13–15). Article II, section 4, of the original city charter (January 15, 1863) explained the scope and duties of the office:

> *It shall be the duty of the city marshal, in addition to the duties prescribed to him by the city council, to execute and return all process issued by the recorder, or directed to him by any legal authority, and attend regularly upon the recorder's court and the meetings of common council; he may appoint one or more deputies who shall possess the same power and authority as the marshal; he shall arrest all persons guilty of a breach of the peace, and of a violation of the city ordinances, and bring them before the recorder for trial, and possess superintending control over the peace and quiet of the city.*

The elective process did not free the office from political meddling. On May 1, 1876, councilman John Menomy (*Hidden History* 66) moved that the marshal be instructed "to desist from making any unnecessary arrests." The marshal in question was Joseph Vincent, who was no novice to law enforcement but was still earning only $5 ($110) a month. He was deputy marshal in March 1865, when the territorial secretary and a detachment of troops from Fort Lapwai forcibly removed government documents from the territorial prison on First Street. He was later a judge and played a pivotal role in the investigation of the murders of Chinese miners in Deep Creek, Oregon, in May 1887.

The first reference to a "policeman" in the council minutes appears on April 15, 1879, when George Young was appointed to assist marshal Charles Faunce. Marshals were saddled with following up on city council directives to keep the streets clear of obstructions, collect delinquent taxes and abate "nuisances," as defined by the council. The city did not get around to the idea of licensing "saloons, drinking shops and bar rooms" until August 8,

1881, when Ordinance 41 failed to pass. Ordinance 37, which mandated dog tags, passed muster in July, but the plan to license drinking establishments did not. That which is not regulated needs no policing.

It is small wonder that most marshals served only one term. Faunce was elected twice and resigned twice. Maybe the final straw was his inability to prevent a mob from breaking into the jail to get at Peter Walker, whom it promptly hanged. At least the city began offering more money for the job. In July 1882, the marshal's salary was raised to $50 ($1,100) a month, but pay raises bring increased expectations. The council suspended the pay for C.A. Brisbin in January 1889 until he made a full report on city licenses and taxes. Brisbin complied and then told the council in March to "take this job and shove it." The longest-serving town marshal during the period from 1861 to 1901 was John Roos (1894–99).

Charles Faunce, 1903. *From* The Illustrated History of North Idaho.

Since 1901, the city council has hired the chief of police, who was originally under the direction of the police judge and a city council member who was also police commissioner. The method of selection alleviated a few problems and created a raft of others. If a marshal ran afoul of the residents, they could deny his reelection. After 1901, the whims of the city council trumped reason on several occasions, as we will see in this book. Lewiston city councils have been known, at times, to become contentious, dysfunctional and obstructive.

The minutes from the council's meeting on July 6, 1900, are very revealing. The members approved a set of rules and orders of business recommended to them by a select committee. Rule 12 read, "Any member who is about to speak shall rise from his seat and respectfully address the presiding officer and shall confine himself to the questioning debate and avoid personalities." While the rule may seem to have been instituted for controlling those

Clyde Carpenter, night chief, 1904. *Courtesy of the Lewiston Police Department.*

attending a city council meeting, the intent of the recommendation clearly applied to councilmen, who often sparred publicly over matters. Police chiefs have always had to keep someone happy. However, some chiefs came under as much suspicion as the criminals.

James Hayes was chief of police from 1907 to 1909. In April 1909, a wealthy Lewiston businessman claimed that Hayes had conspired with two vaudevillians to shake him down and induce him "to put up a large sum of money to prevent publicity." The police had entered a hotel room "on a tip" that Leslie Porter (*Historic Firsts* 110–112) would be found in a compromising state with Dorothy Penner. It was all a fraud concocted by Hayes meant to harass Porter.

Penner was instructed to feign sickness to gain entrance to Porter's room and then lie down on his bed. An officer waited outside just long enough for Dorothy to arrange her peignoir. Porter must have really stepped on some important toes for the police to go to such lengths. A jury convicted him of adultery, which had been a crime only since February 1905. Even Mayor Henry Heitfeld (*Historic Firsts* 94) testified against him, saying that Porter could not be depended on to tell the truth. In her deposition, Penner rebutted the state's accusations, holding steadfastly to her claims that Hayes and other city officials had fabricated the whole scheme. Porter got the last laugh. In October 1922, he sold his forty acres east of town to the Clearwater Timber Company for $80,000 ($11.2 million).

Hayes' successor—Abbott "Ab" Masters—drew the ire of Mayor Benjamin Tweedy in early April 1910, when he fired an experienced officer

Benjamin Tweedy, circa 1910. *Courtesy of the City of Lewiston.*

to save money. Tweedy used his authority under the city charter to dismiss Masters and select a new chief. Lewiston now had only three policemen: one for the day shift, one for the night shift and the chief. Masters' firing set off a firestorm, but one councilman agreed with the reduction in force, contending that several years earlier, when Lewiston had "twenty-four or twenty-five saloons, three policemen handled the work, and the city got along all right." Lewiston had two police chiefs, one backed by the mayor and one by the city council. Tweedy told the council that he had "an unlimited number of suspension orders" and would use one every time the council returned Masters to his office. However, when more than three hundred voters signed petitions for Tweedy's recall and Masters' reinstatement, Tweedy blinked.

The suspension was finally lifted on April 19, but the public was less than impressed. On April 18, the *Lewiston Morning Tribune* announced, under the headline "Will Be No Sin," the formation of the Nez Perce County Law Enforcement League at the local Baptist church. More than $14,000 ($350,000) in subscriptions flowed in for enforcement of the local option law, which banned liquor sales in the county. The executive board selected H.L. Butler, who had recently resigned as a Lewiston police officer, as its "secret service agent."

The brouhaha over the Masters affair embarrassed Tweedy, but not as much as what happened on March 18, 1912, when he was vying to be the Republican candidate for Idaho governor. The local Presbyterian church (*Historic Firsts* 63) sponsored a meeting to discuss the upcoming local option election, which would again decide whether Nez Perce County would be

Main and Second Streets, circa 1916. *Courtesy of Special Collections and Archives, University of Idaho Library, 1-28-86-7.*

wet or dry. Officer Thomas Tabor attempted to eject a local prohibition opponent and set off "a riot." Tweedy's wife, Elzora, assaulted Tabor, hitting him in the eye as he tried to quell the disturbance.

Until the 1930s, police officers had no special training for their job. Even city firemen acted as policemen until World War I. Lester Rawls, who grew up in Lewiston in the late 1930s and early 1940s, noted that "they were just policemen because they couldn't find any other job." Men entered the force from diverse and unrelated backgrounds. A case in point was Eugene Gasser, who ran an automobile dealership and was a volunteer fireman before joining the force in 1915 and rising to chief in 1919. He would hold the position longer than any other man in Lewiston's history and become the subject of many stories now firmly embedded in city folklore (*Hidden History* 97–98).

Did Lewiston law enforcement and the city council look the other way or act selectively when criminal activity raised its head in the city? Most certainly, especially when it involved prostitution, gambling and alcohol. Too many anecdotes indicate that the police department would frequently set its own rules or follow less-than-legal dictates from the city council.

A Lewiston taxi driver in the 1920s related that he was called to the Bollinger Hotel (*Hidden History* 40) to pick up a client. Upon checking with the front desk, he learned that no one had made a call from the hotel. Getting

Lewiston and Nez Perce County law enforcement officers, 1927. Seated, second from left, is the county sheriff, Harry Dent. To his left is Lewiston police chief Eugene Gasser. *Courtesy of the Joan Gasser Ely Family Archives.*

back into his cab, he noticed that a small flask of whiskey had been slipped under his visor. He was no dummy. It was Prohibition. He quickly disposed of the flask and prepared to return to the taxi depot on Fourth Street. As he rounded the corner from D Street to approach Main, he was pulled over by Eugene Gasser and a patrolman. Gasser ordered him out of the car, and an unsuccessful search ensued. For whom was the sting intended—the driver or the taxi company? It was an era rife with shenanigans and deviousness. Gasser resigned unexpectedly in May 1941.

In September, within weeks of his departure, Norman Harstad—an inspector for the Berkeley, California police department since 1926—was hired to completely reorganize the department under a six-month contract paying him $275 ($4,400) a month. He had just completed a reorganization of the police department in Palm Springs, California. Harstad was a troubleshooter, and Lewiston had troubles that needed to be rooted out. In October, he instituted a "school of instruction" for Lewiston officers. Not everyone was pleased. Within five months of Harstad's arrival, eight members of the force resigned, including Bud Huddleston, who would later be elected to several terms as Nez Perce County sheriff.

The leadership of the police department became an issue again in 1954. On April 13, the city council met before a packed house to discuss whether it should dismiss Robert Flood, who had been chief since Frank Jacobs had been forced out because of his campaign against the city's complicity with organized prostitution. As a result of the controversy, a fourteen-point policy was adopted to again reorganize the operations of the department. Flood resigned to become a security officer for the atomic energy operations in Idaho Falls.

In January 1960, Floyd Rosecrans gave up after a month-long debate over his handling of the department. He had dismissed a police sergeant, raised the pay of four policemen without authority and, according to the council, allowed internal friction to develop. He fired four of the five women working for the force. Rosecrans' successor, Clyde Dailey, fared little better. So contentious was the debate over his firing of Lieutenant Edward Delp that six members of the council walked out on Mayor Marvin Dean when he tried to bring up the matter on December 6. Lewiston would not see another long-serving police chief until 1962, when William "Bill" Siler took the post from Dailey and remained until 1975.

Let's be fair: Lewiston has been, for a good deal of its history, an ornery and undisciplined town. It was far from an easy task to uphold the law, especially when the police were often the targets of criminals. As pointed out in *Historic Firsts*, more Lewiston policemen have died in the line of duty than in any department in Idaho.

In his book *Selling Your Father's Bones: America's 140-Year War Against the Nez Perce Tribe*, Brian Schofield asserts that from its beginnings, "Lewiston was a profoundly challenging place to love." Lester Rawls recounted, "The town never slept. It was just going all the time." When Rawls was stationed in Japan during the occupation after World War II, his sergeant asked him where he hailed from. Upon hearing "Lewiston, Idaho," the career sergeant exclaimed, "That's the wildest town I was ever in!"

Lois Jacksha, a retired credit analyst for several downtown Lewiston stores in the 1940s and 1950s, observed, "A neighbor told us that if a marriage could survive Lewiston, it could survive anything." As you will soon learn, some marriages ended, not with a whimper but with a bang. All human relationships are fragile under the best of circumstances.

No individual account in this book occurred without leaving marks on untold and unnamed others. History paints with a broad brush and does not stay inside the lines.

Never think you've seen the last of anything.
—*Eudora Welty*

1

A Town of Negotiable Virtue

You can make prostitution illegal, but you can't make it unpopular.
—*Martin Berhman*

The armies slaughtering one another in the East during the Civil War had their hordes of camp followers, often the wives and children of soldiers; liquor salesmen; and hookers, a term popularized by its association with the Army of the Potomac, commanded for a time by General Joseph "Fighting Joe" Hooker. Civil War historian Bruce Catton related that a red-light district in Washington, D.C., was known as "Hooker's Division." There was a time when most of downtown Lewiston was a red-light district, but let us begin at the beginning.

When the riverboat *Colonel Wright* steamed its way up the Snake River in May 1861, the confluence with the Clearwater was not its destination. Commanded by Leonard White, the boat pushed up the Clearwater to the Big Eddy bend in the river near present-day Lenore. The spring runoff made mooring the boat very dangerous. Proponents of the new town of Slaterville gave up and moved downstream to a more favorable location, which was called Ragtown because of its tent-city appearance. According to the June 6, 1895 *Lewiston Teller*, the steamer *Okanagon* was tied up at the confluence on June 1, 1861, when it was suggested that the new landing should have a proper name. Many options were offered, but Victor Trevitt's recommendation of "Lewiston," in honor of Meriwether Lewis, won approval.

Leonard Wright, circa 1860. *From* Lewis & Dryden's Marine History of the Pacific Northwest *(1895)*.

An old American mining camp adage states, "First came the miners to work in the mine. Next came the ladies who lived on the line." In the spring of 1862, White scheduled a return trip to Lewiston, this time with a much different passenger list. In *Blow for the Landing: A Hundred Years of Steam Navigation on the Waters of the West*, Fritz Timmen describes the scene as White waited at the mouth of the Walla Walla River for the ice to break up on the Snake after the harsh winter:

[The *Colonel Wright* was] *burdened with all the plunder necessary to build and equip a first-class saloon, gambling hall, and honky-tonk. The passenger list was liberally sprinkled with gamblers, bartenders, and an attractive collection of dance-hall hostesses and vaudeville entertainers...The word spread among the woman-hungry bachelors on nearby ranches that the* Wright's *most important cargo wore perfume. The boat was besieged. In panic, Captain White cast off for the more isolated shelter of Ice Harbor. His strategy failed. By canoe, raft, and rowboat, amorous single males for miles around sought out the steamer. By the time the troupe was delivered at Lewiston, its manager had to send back to Portland for additional female personnel. But ranch life in Franklin, Whitman, and Walla Walla counties was a lot less lonely from then on.*

For many women, prostitution presented itself as a safety net in a world without social services. Famed outlaw Henry Plummer (*Hidden History* 98) stayed in Lewiston from time to time in the early 1860s during lulls in his career as a hoodlum on the one hand and as a sheriff on the other. By one account, his mistress accompanied him. She had deserted her husband and three children in Walla Walla to take up with

Plummer. During one of their stays, Henry regrouped with former ne'er-do-well associates and abandoned her to renew his highwayman pursuits elsewhere when local vigilantes began to focus their attention on his activities. She turned to prostitution to feed herself and the two children she had given birth to while with Plummer, finally dying an alcoholic in one of Lewiston's worst bordellos.

The identities of those first "fallen doves" remain elusive and are most often mentioned as minor characters in the tumult that surrounded Lewiston's early days. A case in point is the sad story of Billy Page, who had turned state's evidence in the prosecution of the killers of Lloyd Magruder and his companions in October 1863. Billy's life had gone south since the trial and execution (*History Firsts* 47–48). He was earning his keep by carrying water from the Clearwater to the brothel where Albert Igo, a short-tempered villain, was cavorting with the "sporting women," a reference to their working in gambling halls. Igo got very drunk and was severely beaten by Page after an argument. In the summer of 1867, Billy came to work and found his favorite prostitute, Eliza Wilson, "making the beast with two backs" with Igo. In a rage, Billy attacked Al, who grabbed his shotgun and blew Billy's head off. The coroner's inquest ruled it was murder, but no trial was ever held.

The next mentions of Lewiston prostitutes by name appear in the 1870 Idaho death index and the 1870 federal census. The index lists Li Hoy as dying from syphilis on an unspecified date before the publication of the registry. As Chinese settlers did not reach Lewiston until at least 1864, she would have died at some point in that window, probably not more than thirty years of age.

Death from syphilis occurs in the tertiary (final) stage, which can follow the initial infection by three to fifteen years. Li Hoy undoubtedly contracted the disease before arriving in Lewiston and infected countless men. She may also have become quite disfigured. Pockets of damage (lesions) are concentrated in various tissues, such as the bones, skin, nervous tissue, heart and arteries, creating what are called "gummas," tumors having a rubbery consistency.

Lewiston was a town where women had become financially independent. Carlotta Felis and Anna Ream were listed as prostitutes in the 1870 census. That was no economic barrier for them. The census credited Felis with assets amounting to $1,400 ($26,500) and Ream with $1,500 ($28,500). An 1872 taxpayers survey of the wealthiest individuals in Nez Perce County (which, at the time, took in most of northern Idaho) showed that

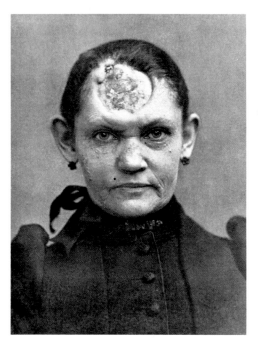

Facial gumma. *From* A Practical Treatise on Diseases of the Skin *(1892)*.

many prominent men and some businesses could not match the women's wealth. A careful reading of the census data shows that Carlotta's daughter Julia was attending Lewiston's public school, as were the children of other prostitutes.

Madams and prostitutes of the nineteenth century became some of the most librated women of their time. They enjoyed a level of personal freedom, wealth and education unknown to the vast majority of American women, who would not think of consorting with a man of another race, walking alone in public or wearing makeup. Thaddeus Russell provides us with another perspective on the lives of prostitutes in his book *A Renegade History of the United States*:

In fact, prostitutes won virtually all the freedoms that were denied to women but are now taken for granted. Prostitutes were especially successful in the wild, lawless, thoroughly renegade boomtowns of the West. When women were barred from most jobs and wives had no legal right to own property, madams in the West owned large tracts of land and prized real estate. Prostitutes made, by far, the highest wages of all American women. Several madams were so wealthy that they funded irrigation and road-building projects that laid the foundation for the New West. Decades before American employers offered health insurance to their workers, madams across the West provided their employees with free health care. While women were told that they could not and should not protect themselves from violence, and wives had no legal recourse against being raped by their husbands, police officers were employed by madams to protect the women who worked for them, and many madams owned and knew how to use guns.

Prim Victorian wives and early feminists were unlikely to admit it, but, aside from the sexual aspects of the prostitute's trade, you can almost hear them thinking, "You go, girl!" If a woman wanted to strike out on her own and cast off the corseted conventions of American life after the Civil War, the rough-and-tumble economy and demographic mishmash in the West was a tempting lure to freethinking women. Their major hurdle would be the eventual civilizing of the West. That would happen gradually, and Lewiston was no exception.

Lewiston's original city charter did address prostitution, although with different terminology. Article 5 asserted:

> *The mayor and common council shall have power within the city to license, tax, restrain, prohibit, and suppress billiard tables, tipling* [sic] *houses, gaming and gambling houses and houses of ill-fame.*

In *Selling Your Father's Bones*, Schofield asserts that after the bloom of the gold rush had faded, "Lewiston's sole growth industries were now prostitution and corruption." There is no evidence that prostitution was in any way regulated until April 15, 1879, when the city council passed Ordinance 26, which ordered the suppression of "nuisances." The town's odd sensibilities and priorities can be no better exemplified than by the fact that city fathers had begun restricting swine, horses and cattle from running at large in July 1876. The limitations of Ordinance 26 quickly became apparent, and the council readdressed the issue on August 19, amending section one to include within its prohibitions "all houses, saloons or Bar rooms within the corporate limits of the City, and not merely on E or Montgomery Streets" (original names for Main Street). It was the first attempt to place restrictions on brothels, but declaring a bordello to be a nuisance is not the same as closing it. The geographical tone of the legislation would take on new significance as the years passed.

With houses of prostitution so prevalent that legislation focused only on their location, one has to wonder how residents coped with the situation in everyday life. There were some unspoken accommodations. Parents ordered their children to never be within speaking distance of a prostitute. Local businessmen developed an order-and-deliver system to keep prostitutes out of their stores, sending out samples by courier for the madams' selection. No girls plied their trade on the sidewalks. On occasion, the local newspaper would carry an indignant letter from a reader, as was the case in the August 2, 1878 issue of the *Lewiston Teller*:

The Angus Trimble Saloon, circa 1880. *Courtesy of Special Collections and Archives, University of Idaho Library, 5-007-4b.*

We should like to ask your city government if they are aware that houses of prostitution are being kept open in broad daylight on the public thoroughfare of your city. If they are aware of it, do they take pleasure listening to the filthy language that is used by the wretches who congregate in front of certain saloons? It is about time that the respectable people of our community took the matter in hand.

Brothels in frontier towns like Lewiston housed only a few women, usually numbering no more than five or six. Each woman rented her room from a madam who owned or leased the building and was required to split her fees with the madam. Prostitutes kept their tips. Some houses issued chits, which were tokens serving as cash for drinks, food and sexual favors. The use of chits by local businesses, such as the Seraphin Wildenthaler Bakery, was a common practice in the town for many years.

In 1888, when the local Chinese community began soliciting funds to build the Beuk Aie Miao temple, nineteen businesses contributed, one of which had a distinctly feminine name, Xing-xiang-guan ("Fragrance of Apricot

Gallery"), likely identifying it as a brothel. Six Chinese women donated funds ranging from $0.50 ($13) to $5 ($130), and their first names appear on the donor boards, including those of Ronghui and Yongji. According to the last local Chinese elder who lived in Lewiston at the beginning of the twentieth century, the listing of only the women's first names would have prevented embarrassment for their families. Their being able to donate funds in their own names indicates that they were not slaves as we would envision slavery. County census records from the territorial period do identify some Chinese women as prostitutes, but the designation may have been a cultural bias. Immigration and census officials routinely suspected that single Chinese women were prostitutes (*Historic Firsts* 82–83).

The issue of prostitution does not reappear in the minutes of the council until August 4, 1890, when city attorney Jonathan Howe (*Lost Lewiston* 62) was instructed to draft a statue to amend Ordinance 26 to include church and school blocks. Passed on August 15, Ordinance 118 restricted the locations of brothels in the city but did not outlaw the practice of prostitution. The ordinance had limited and isolated effects, for the city school and three of its five churches (Presbyterian, Methodist and Episcopalian) were located in the same block (*Historic Firsts* 63; *Lost Lewiston* 58, 81). Howe would have readily accepted the assignment, being a member of the Universalist congregation meeting at Seventh and Main Streets. Without doubt, Father Alexander Diomedi wanted to clear the area around St. Stanislaus Church and St. Aloysius School on Fifth Street, near the heaviest concentration of brothels. Prostitution was going to be tolerated, but not in certain neighborhoods, much like adult bookstores in many communities today.

Lewiston was experiencing a case of moral uncertainty. On October 14, 1895, the council repealed Ordinance 46, which dated from August 1881 and provided for the closing of all shops on Sundays other than those engaged in the sale of "bread, fresh meat, or drugs, or hotels and restaurants." Many city hotels soon had blocks of hotel rooms strangely booked by the hour each and every day. The madams found a way to keep their clients happy and their bank accounts full. An unverified report states that the first time an American woman smoked a cigarette in public was in the dining room of the newly opened Bollinger Hotel about 1900. There can be little doubt that she was a local madam who liked her Ogden's Guinea Golds.

The moral pendulum began to swing again in early 1896. In January, city attorney James Poe (*Lost Lewiston* 116) began drafting legislation to prohibit women from frequenting saloons. The "women" in question were clearly not the likes of Sarah Vollmer, Anna McConkey and Harriet

Lewiston's red-light district north of C Street (foreground at the confluence), 1899. *Courtesy of the Nez Perce County Historical Society.*

Morris. Poe presented Ordinance 195 to the council for passage on February 3. In November 1897, a petition reached the council, calling on the body to prohibit gambling within the city limits. Few Lewiston businessmen signed the petition, and it was returned for further study. When the petition was resubmitted in December, it was quickly tabled, and gambling remained a dependable source of city revenue until the early 1950s (*Hidden History* 128).

Sometime in early 1898, a "committee on houses of ill-fame" began its work, and the report of a resulting survey gives us an important clue about how prevalent the houses were throughout the community. On March 7, the committee reported that "in their present location and conditions, [the bordellos were] a menace to the good order and morals of the City and conducted in a very disreputable manner." Just what a brothel could do to make itself reputable in the town's eyes was never explained. Acting on the orders of the council, Poe presented Ordinance 223 for passage, requiring "all such houses to be located north of C Street." The statute aimed to "restrain and suppress" prostitution, but stopping it altogether would take more thought and courage.

On rare occasions, the goings-on in a Lewiston brothel appeared in local newspapers. Such was the case in March 1898. William Redding died in a bordello on Fourth Street. He had been in town for about a week. He sold out his interest in a sawmill on the Salmon River and arrived in Lewiston with $800 ($23,000) in cash, a team of horses and a wagon and told everyone that he was on his way to the Klondike.

Shortly after arriving, he went on a weeklong bender. During his spree, he gambled off or squandered all but $200 ($5,600) of his funds. Redding finally decided to resume his journey north but wanted one more evening sampling Lewiston's nightlife. He accompanied Mattie Williams, a local "sporting woman," back to her room on Fourth Street, a room that a newspaper account described as a "dive." At 4:00 a.m., "Doc" Williams, Mattie's pimp, found Redding near death. Williams called a physician, but the man was dead before help arrived. The coroner took charge but declined to perform an autopsy, as there was no evidence of foul play.

The council ultimately acted on August 14, 1899, with the passage of Ordinance 248, sections of which are well worth reading:

AN ORDINANCE TO SUPPRESS HOUSES OF ILL-FAME AND PROSTITUTION AND TO PROVIDE A PENALTY FOR ITS VIOLATION

The City of Lewiston does ordain as follows:

SECTION 1. That all dissolute women and other disreputable persons found strolling or loitering about any street, alley or public place in the City of Lewiston, after ten o'clock P.M., and any female who shall be guilty of soliciting prostitution upon any of the streets, alleys or public spaces within the city shall upon conviction be punished by a fine of not less than five dollars [$145 today] nor more than fifty dollars [$1,450], and costs of prosecution.

SEC. 2. Whoever shall keep and maintain within the corporate limits of the City of Lewiston bawdy houses, houses of ill-fame, or any place for the practice of fornication or prostitution or shall knowingly furnish any building, room or part thereof or any place reserved by him or her as under his or her control to be used for that purpose shall upon conviction be fined in the sum of not less than five dollars nor more than fifty dollars and costs of prosecution.

SEC. 3. That any person who may be found guilty of any offense under this ordinance shall be confined in the city jail until the fine which may be imposed and the costs are paid at the rate of two dollars per day.

A policy of "fine and release" would remain in effect for fifty years. Madams and prostitutes were formally disenfranchised under the provisions of the city charter and code. However, as with all legislation, the proof was in the enforcement. In December 1900, the Sanborn Map Company returned to Lewiston to update its plates of the growing town.

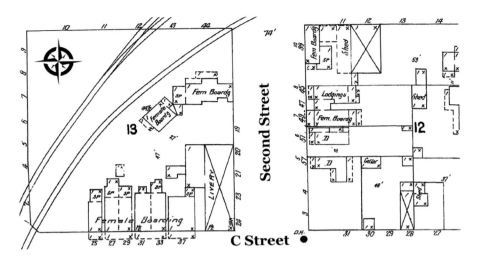

Detail from the December 1900 Sanborn map, plate two. *Courtesy of the Branting Archives.*

The company had surveyed the city in 1888, 1891 and 1896. Plate two of the 1896 set had shown two "female boarding houses," both of which were located in Chinatown on First Street. The 1900 updates told the whole truth. The neighborhood of Second and C Streets had no fewer than ten bordellos. A key to understanding how Lewiston was not unlike other American communities can be found in *United States History*, Volume 2:

> *Every major city and most small towns had their own vice districts where prostitution, gambling, and other illicit activities proliferated. These districts were usually restricted to one of the older and centrally located neighborhoods where upper- or middle-class families no longer resided. For this reason, vice was often tolerated by city authorities so long as it confined itself to these boundaries. Vice was profitable for urban political machines that relied on bribes and the occasional fines they collected through raids. These limited attempts at enforcement filled city coffers and presented the impression of diligence…In fact, most prostitution dens were located near police stations.*

Ordinance 223, although repealed, had effectively created a red-light district. Lewiston's Johns did not need to walk all over town. When the November 1904 Sanborn maps were published, brothels lined both sides of C Street between First and Second Streets. By the publication of the November 1909 plates, the number had grown to eighteen separate

The old *Lewiston Morning Tribune* building and later the site of the Beevers Hotel, 1898. *Courtesy of the* Lewiston Tribune.

buildings, all within one block of one another. The police station was one block away on Third Street, and any policeman could show you the correct way to fold a dollar bill to gain entrance to a brothel without being hassled. The police department's arrest ledgers for 1905–06 list many prostitutes—Florence Thompson, Esther Large, Ruth Smith, among others—along with a number of their pimps. They all paid $7 ($180) fines right on schedule at the end of each month. By World War I, the situation had dramatically changed. The old ramshackle, stick-frame brothels were gone, and the madams had moved into more comfortable brick-and-mortar lodgings on Main Street.

This apparent city cleanup came in the wake of external factors. The entry of young women into the workforce of most cities made them financially and morally independent, and this independence frightened moral conservatives. Rumors abounded that women were being forced into prostitution and moved like pawns around the United States and overseas by cabals managed by nefarious immigrants. The term "white slavery" entered the public consciousness and elicited a nationwide knee-jerk reaction. Muckraking journalists did little to quell the furor, filling newspapers with

Mabel Harris, aka Mae Rivers, circa 1900. *Courtesy of Bonnie Sanders.*

lurid tales of how innocent girls had been kidnapped off the streets, drugged, smuggled around the country and forced into servitude in brothels. Modern research fails to verify any of the claims.

The legislative product of the hysteria was the Mann Act, signed into law by President William Howard Taft in 1910. The law made it a crime to transport women across state lines "for the purpose of prostitution or debauchery, or for any other immoral purpose." As Lewiston is a state border town, federal law officials began to look closely at the community, as we shall see.

In December 1903, Lewiston was witness to a revealing court decision. Judge Edgar Steele (*Historic Firsts* 118) ruled in the case of *Hirselberger v. Schumacher*, a slander suit in the amount of $10,000 ($250,000). Cimma Hirselberger claimed that Schumaker had told him she was a prostitute. Judge Steele dismissed the suit on the grounds that adultery and prostitution were not offenses under any Idaho statute. As late as 1972, the Idaho Code still had no statute forbidding prostitution, only the activities associated with it, whatever those were.

The 300 block of Main Street became the site of several brothels: the Grand Hotel, the Antlers Hotel, the Luna House Hotel, the Savoy Hotel and the Oxford Annex. Mabel Harris appeared in Lewiston about 1900 and would eventually own several hotels, including the Imperial and the Luna House Hotel. She visited the surrounding mining camps to drum up business. Her business card for the Luna House Hotel read, "In the Center of the Business District. Mabel Harris, 307 Main Street, Lewiston, Idaho. Strictly Modern. Your Patronage Solicited. Rates Reasonable."

Arriving in Lewiston in 1907, fellow madam Louise Cordelia "Lou" Beevers (also known as "Madam Lou") owned the Beevers and the Vendrome (604 Main Street). The Beevers and the Oxford Rooms, at one time, were located in the building that is now the new Lewiston City Library.

The *Lewiston Tribune* hired Thomas J. Campbell away from a competing newspaper in 1909. Known for his dark suits and starched collars, Campbell became an icon among Pacific Northwest editors. The newspaper's offices and printing facilities were located on Fourth Street, next to the Mark Means Building, the second floor of which was a notable Lewiston brothel.

In August 1921, Thomas and his wife, Lora, were blessed with their only child, Thomas W., whom most people knew as "Little Tom." Both parents were reporters, with Lora writing society columns for the *Tribune*. What do working parents do with a small child? Get

Louise "Lou" Beevers, circa 1907. *Courtesy of Elaine Booth.*

29

The Mark Means Building, before 1909. *Courtesy of the Nez Perce County Historical Society.*

Lewiston State Normal School kindergarten play, 1928. "Little Tom" Campbell is kneeling second from the left. *Courtesy of Connie Hyke Bekavac and Gwen Hyke Horvath.*

a babysitter, of course. His father would take Little Tom next door to the Oxford Rooms. Girls who were not on duty loved caring for the small boy, making up a bed on top of the bordello's pool table as a cozy spot where he could take his naps. And as brothels also served food, Little Tom lacked for nothing and would grow up to be one of Idaho's premier reporters.

Dr. Edward Hoffman began his pre-medicine studies at the University of Idaho in 1932. His fraternity brothers soon sought him out after their weekend visits to Lewiston. Nearly every hotel and boardinghouse on Main Street contained a brothel. Even the Lewis-Clark and Bollinger Hotels were involved. Elevator operators and taxi drivers had girls "on call." Clients found the "black" brothel on D Street, one block from Brackenbury Square. While a few prostitutes grew up in or around Lewiston, most were part of a circuit that ran from the West Coast, through eastern Washington and into north Idaho. Hoffman knew at least two Lewiston physicians who were regularly performing abortions.

His first long-term assignment after his graduation brought him to Lewiston in 1937 to work at the Public Health Department office, located in the basement of the county courthouse. In August 1939, the city's police department began fingerprinting women living in the downtown "rooming houses." Chief Eugene Gasser was responding to pressure from the FBI. A recent raid netted three women and three men, who were taken into custody on suspicion of violating the Mann Act. By the eleventh of the month, five more women had been fingerprinted, while others were ordered to appear at the police station. Local newspaper coverage made no mention of prostitution. The police were focusing on men who had "no means of livelihood"—you know, pimps.

Lewiston's health regulations required prostitutes to submit to blood tests. Dr. Hoffman also gave health lectures at the Bollinger Hotel as a public

Dr. Edward Hoffman, 1944. *Courtesy of the Nez Perce County Historical Society.*

service. One of every twenty samples was proving to be positive. At one lecture, when he offered to take samples, the men started to walk out. On another evening, he had a difficult time keeping the men's attention as a prostitute in a brothel across the street in what is now Morgan's Alley did a striptease on a stairwell landing.

While the exact number of Lewiston prostitutes is unknown, Judith Walkowitz's book *Prostitution and Victorian Society* provides an intriguing statistic. She discovered that one of every 36 residents of London was a prostitute in 1910. Lewiston's population in 1910 was 6,100, yielding a staggering result of 170 prostitutes. By 1930, 250 prostitutes may well have been found in Lewiston and the Orchards, which would soon become a center for the business.

The level of paradigm blindness (*Lost Lewiston* 149–150) among Lewiston residents is no better explained than with an anecdote from a meeting Dr. Hoffman had with what was most likely the Tsceminicum Club, Lewiston's most select women's organization. Upon learning how prevalent prostitution was, members wanted to know what could be done. Hoffman told them the truth: their husbands—many of whom were city council members, doctors, lawyers and prominent businessmen—owned the buildings where prostitution was thriving under police protection. Some of the doyennes had a sudden case of "the vapors." A longtime Lewiston clothier recalled his embarrassment when local civic leaders would visit his store with their wives while wearing ties that prostitutes had purchased from his stock and given them as gifts.

The issue reached a crisis on July 18, 1942, when Chief Petty Officer M.E. Cornelius recommended that navy trainees at the University of Idaho radio school should no longer be allowed liberty in Lewiston, whose leaders were stonewalling him. Again, no one used the word "prostitution," but there was little doubt about the problem. Supposedly, underage drinking resulted in red-eyed trainees on Monday mornings. Officials from the Army Air Corps base in Walla Walla, Washington, and the Farragut Naval Air Station, near Sandpoint, Idaho, joined Cornelius in demanding a solution. The scope of the problem can be appreciated when one learns that 293,000 servicemen passed through Farragut during the war. The U.S. Navy's second-largest flight training school in the nation was housed at the Clarkston airport and Lewiston State Normal School. More than one thousand naval pilots received their training in Lewiston.

Officials set up a prophylactic station in the Bollinger Hotel, but the infection rate continued to climb. I well remember seeing old stickers

The Hume Hotel, 209 Main Street, circa 1945. *Courtesy of the University of Washington Libraries.*

promoting condoms in a men's room at the college. Lewiston's answer to the problem was all smoke and mirrors. Too much was at stake.

Lacking any authority, Hoffman told the visiting military leaders that the only way to curb the problem was to place the city out-of-bounds.

And so they did, much to the chagrin of the chamber of commerce, whose members said they would tar and feather the person who came up with the idea. Police chief Ed Jacks suspected Hoffman and paid him a visit; "hands off" was the message. Then, Mayor Robert McGregor punctuated the chief's directive. Finally, Idaho governor Chase Clark called to give his formal stamp of disapproval. Hoffman was to make no more statements and was reassigned.

Not to be out-maneuvered by the military, an enterprising madam opened a "roadhouse" at 432 Stewart Avenue in the Orchards (*Lost Lewiston* 139–146). Renovations in the 1990s uncovered a roulette wheel and remnants of slot machines. The bedrooms at the back of the house each had exterior entrances. How many other "roadhouses" existed in the Orchards during the government ban can only be guessed at. The "quarantine" ended in 1946, but Lewiston's reputation had been so damaged by the controversy with the U.S. Army and Navy that doing nothing was no longer an option.

In February 1946, Barent Burhans, the San Francisco field representative for the Federal Security Agency (FSA), commended Lewiston's cooperation with the FSA in wiping out "commercialized vice." The United States was experiencing an upswing in venereal diseases, prostitution and the relaxation of health and law regulations similar to the "social deterioration" after the First World War. His visit must have been a closely choreographed affair. The city council had actually moved in on the pimps and had virtually taken over the territory.

The June 1949 election for seats on the city council turned into a referendum on the subject of managed vice. Justice of the peace James West, a candidate for councilman, contended that, as prostitution existed openly in the city, the practice should be legalized and taxed, making Lewiston an "open city." West was soundly defeated, and Chief Frank Jacobs took the election as a mandate.

On June 14, he finally threw down the gauntlet to Lewiston's red-light district and the city council. In an interview with the press, he asserted that "prostitution has been permitted in the city under the official direction of the city council for the last three years," with his department complicit with the arrangement. Aside from medical examinations and fingerprinting, Lewiston had been issuing certificates declaring local prostitutes to be free of venereal disease, a practice condemned by the Idaho Medical Society and the American Medical Association (AMA). Idaho public health representative James Houser bemoaned the city's continued practice:

Medical control of prostitution is impossible. In fact, it is illegal and unethical for a physician to issue a certificate. The AMA states medical inspection of prostitutes is untrustworthy, inefficient, gives a false sense of security and falls to prevent the spread of infection...In spite of tragedies, city and county officials continue to be hoodwinked by these prostitutes and their pimps and insist that commercialized prostitution be allowed to exist.

Hoffman had learned early on that whatever he did to get diseased prostitutes out of circulation proved to be a waste of time. Homer Brutzman, police chief at the time, asserted that the department had no control over the prostitutes' blood testing. However, he would agree to remove any prostitute who tested positive for a sexually transmitted disease. By Hoffman's estimates, each infected prostitute exposed as many as forty men every week, and he produced positive results for two women. When he performed his follow-up examination, he discovered that the chief had changed the women's names and moved them across the street to another brothel. However, the blood testing campaign so upset the normalcy of the brothel business that several prostitutes moved into apartments on Normal Hill and began working from home.

The influx of what Chief Jacobs called "streetwalkers" prompted the closure of the houses. "It is difficult to arrest these stray women," he reported. "They follow no health rules and are generally filthy." All of the brothels were closed. Jacobs got his way, and then the city council struck back, forcing his resignation in September.

Lewiston was one of three Inland Empire cities that rated among the nation's best in a poll published in the February 12, 1952 issue of *Look* magazine. More than two hundred cities were listed as "good, fair, poor or bad" on the basis of information gathered by undercover agents working for the American Social Hygiene Association. Lewiston was praised as being among the cities having eliminated organized prostitution. Moscow, Spokane and Richland also received "good" ratings. A "bad" score went to Walla Walla, Washington, and Wallace, Idaho. The history of prostitution in Wallace is a story all its own.

Lewiston's new police chief Robert Flood reacted with pride to the *Look* article:

The people of Lewiston want a clean, healthy place to raise their families, and efforts to maintain that will not detract from the attractiveness of Lewiston so far as industry is concerned. I believe reports such as that of Look *magazine are a credit to the citizens of Lewiston and may go a long way toward restoration of our college here.*

Flood added that the Sixth Army headquarters in San Francisco recently advised his office that investigators had labeled Lewiston as "good" in its study of vice conditions throughout the western states. Any connection between the college and organized vice was only in Flood's mind, and in April 1954, he became another casualty of city politics.

The working girls had worn out their Lewiston welcome after nearly ninety years. The madams packed up their belongings and moved to other cities, notably Clarkston, Washington, where cases of brothels disguised as massage parlors continued to generate news stories well into the 1980s. In 1979, the police chief of Lapwai, Idaho, just east of Lewiston, was charged with attempting to induce a woman into prostitution. He could have learned a thing or two from Lewiston officials in the city's not-so-long-ago past.

"IF AT FIRST YOU DON'T SUCCEED"—you know the rest. Well, Andrew Kjeseth proved the axiom's truth the hard way. With a new revolver in his hand and four chambers empty, neighbors found his body in a fence corner in the Orchards on the afternoon of January 17, 1908. There was not much question about what had happened.

Andrew had been living with his sister, Mrs. Nelson Lee, and was complaining that he felt "a slow approach of insanity." A resident of Spokane, Washington, he had been discharged from the hospital in Moscow, Idaho, the previous week after "taking the cure" for alcoholism.

The day before his death, Andrew purchased a new suit of clothes and disposed of his watch and other personal items. A few hours before shooting himself, he bought a revolver at a downtown hardware store and went back to the Orchards to a spot within sight of his sister's home to end his own life. He had a time of it.

Two bullets cut holes through his hat brim, and one must have whistled by his head before the fourth bullet made a suicide out of Andrew Kjeseth.

2
THORNS IN HIS YOUTHFUL FLESH

To be wronged is nothing unless you continue to remember it.
—Confucius

Nursing a grudge is much like slapping your face and expecting the other person to feel it. Someone lives rent-free in your head. Dislike becomes animosity, animosity becomes hatred and hatred destroys the safeguards of reason and compromise. A farming accident in the summer of 1916 set in motion a thought process in the mind of a seventeen-year-old Lewiston boy that would end in a murder, a jailbreak and a bloody barbershop floor at the state penitentiary.

Jewell Richard "Joe" Freng hired on at Lester Gifford's farm for the start of the hay harvest shortly after the Fourth of July. Poor attendance at Lewiston High School had led to his withdrawal from classes two years earlier. He had been working during the spring and summer months, while living with his parents, Christian and Jennie Freng, at their 1445 Main Street home.

Gifford came to Lewiston around 1899 with his parents, who began farming land seven miles east of town. Educated in the city schools, Lester was managing his father's properties by 1912 and purchased his own farmland in 1915, marrying Anna Lena Sulier on February 9, 1916. Anna was four months pregnant by the time of the harvest.

After haying was completed, Gifford assigned Freng to operate a "header," an old reaping machine that was pushed by horses rather than pulled. The modern-day combine gets its configuration from the header. On August 4,

Lester and Anna Gifford, 1916. *Courtesy of the Virginia Gifford Olson Collection.*

Jewell fell through a defective bottom in the header box and was sufficiently injured that he was sent home to recuperate. He asked Gifford to cover medical expenses. When he and his former employer could not reach an agreement, Jewell purchased a .38 Iver Johnson revolver in mid-September, intending to force Gifford to pay his claim.

Jewell entered the old White Hospital (*Lost Lewiston* 42) on September 25 to undergo surgery to repair a rupture stemming from the farm accident and remained there until October 11. Upon his release, he began carrying the revolver on his person at all times. Over the next two months, Jewell threatened Gifford, asserting that he would shoot him if the latter did not pay for his operation and hospital bill, amounting to $130 ($2,700). Gifford denied any responsibility for the accident but offered to pay if a jury were to find him liable. A frail young man who disliked confrontation, Gifford complained to the police of Jewell's persistent demands. Anna had recently given birth to a daughter, Mary Virginia. It was only a matter of time until the two young men met in public. The safeguards of reason and compromise had long since been breached.

On Saturday, December 16, at about 5:30 p.m., Jewell saw Lester, with Anna and baby Mary Virginia, driving his buggy on Main Street. The streets were crowded with people busily doing their Christmas shopping. Jewell approached and asked Lester what he was going to do about the hospital

Right: Mary Virginia Gifford, 1917. *Courtesy of the Virginia Gifford Olson Collection.*

Below: The Idanha Pharmacy (left) and the intersection of Main and New Sixth Streets, circa 1926. *Courtesy of the Nez Perce County Historical Society.*

bill. Freng later related that Lester's answer was "unsatisfactory." From that point, all bets were off. Jewell told Lester that he could take his choice: pay the bill or die. He pulled the Iver Johnson from his pocket to ensure that Lester knew how serious he was. Composing himself, Lester explained that he did not have a checkbook and would have to step into a nearby store to prepare a bank draft. He knew that if Jewell became violent, Anna and their baby girl would be in the line of fire.

The nearest store was the Idanha Pharmacy, owned by Christian Osmers (*Lost Lewiston* 38) and located on the southwest corner of Main and Park Way (now New Sixth Street).

Jewell followed Lester into the store, where a clerk provided a blank draft. The two men moved to the cash register at the end of the soda fountain, attracting no particular attention until Lester caught Osmers' attention and called him over, at which time he explained that Freng was forcing him to sign a check at gunpoint. Gifford wanted Osmers' advice about what he should do and, of course, to have a witness to the extortion.

Osmers later testified that physical violence was imminent and that he told the men they had to leave his store if such was going to be the case. Lester requested that someone call the police. Jewell immediately made it known that neither the pharmacist nor his clerk should interfere or "there would be something doing." Osmers counseled Gifford to sign the check, stating that it would be worthless if obtained under such circumstances. He even offered to serve as a witness to the felonious transaction.

Christian Osmers, circa 1940. *Courtesy of the City of Lewiston.*

The three men continued to parley for a few minutes, with Osmers attempting to defuse the confrontation. All the time, Jewell kept repeating in a low and deliberate voice that if any police or other persons attempted to interfere, serious consequences would ensue. Gifford signed the check and handed it to Jewell. At that moment, Lewiston policeman Eugene Gasser entered the pharmacy. Upon seeing the officer, Jewell leveled his gun and pulled the trigger. Gifford had turned away and was attempting to escape behind the soda fountain. Jewell's first shot entered Gifford's back below his left shoulder, passing directly through his heart. He was dead before he hit the floor.

Jewell turned his attention to Osmers, who attempted to grasp him by the arm and divert his aim. The cash register got in his way, and Jewell was able to get off one shot. The bullet passed through the left sleeve of Osmers' coat, between the elbow and the shoulder, narrowly missing his arm.

Lester Gifford, circa 1911. *Courtesy of the Virginia Gifford Olson Collection.*

Gasser rushed Jewell and succeeded in holding his arms down to his sides, as Jewell continued to shoot, three bullets going into the floor behind the soda fountain. How had Gasser known that things were afoot at the Idanha?

Leslie Houchens, an employee at the nearby Madison Lumber Company, had witnessed the trouble between Gifford and Jewell in the street. After Jewell forced Gifford from the buggy and into the Idanha at the point of his revolver, Houchens took charge of the horse-and-carriage, trying to comfort a distraught Anna. He then ran to the Star Dray Company office on Park Way and telephoned the police station about a quarter mile away. Gasser responded in a police car and, upon arriving, was advised that a man inside the pharmacy had a gun and was going to kill someone.

Within minutes of the shooting, a mass of gawking onlookers crowded in front of the pharmacy. Jewell was arrested immediately and quickly transported to the county jail, which was then a separate building behind the courthouse on Thirteenth Street. Jewell's father and one of his sisters visited the jail that evening, but the cellblock was locked by the time they arrived. His father returned with Jewell's cousin early the next morning but did not see him until nearly 10:00 a.m. Jewell showed little interest in

Eugene Gasser, circa 1937. *Courtesy of the Joan Gasser Ely Family Archives.*

their presence, barely speaking with his cousin. He spoke with his father for perhaps a minute that day, doing so in such a low tone that officers could not make out what was said. The young Freng then indicated that he wanted to return to his cell.

When he was booked into the jail, Jewell had been buoyant, thinking that Gifford had only been wounded. Upon learning the truth the next morning, his demeanor changed dramatically. Initially, his father was highly agitated, telling the officers at the courthouse that he would rather see his son dead than where he was now. By Saturday evening, the shock had worn off, but the reality of his son's situation was still apparent. Families were caught up in a maelstrom. Anna was a widow with a five-week-old baby girl. She buried Lester on Tuesday, December 19, in the Knights of Pythias section of Normal Hill Cemetery, after a funeral at the old Vassar Funeral Home on Ninth Street (*Historic Firsts* 114).

Jewell's sister Julia collapsed when she heard of her brother's arrest. In failing health from appendicitis, Julia journeyed to Spokane in early January 1917 for medical treatment. She died suddenly on January 8. Attending physician J.M. Powell was quoted as saying, "The shock of her brother's affair in Lewiston was largely responsible for her death."

A trial was months away. The Idaho state legislature had just created the Tenth Judicial District, and the new judge, Wallace N. Scales, had yet to be qualified and seated, which would occur in early April.

Jewell spoke to few people over the next months, but after his sister's death, things changed. Nate Rogers was arrested on January 17 on charges of supplying liquor to the Nez Perce Reservation and defaulting on his bond in the federal court in Moscow. Hal Burton was locked up on March 4 after being arrested for stealing wheat from a rail car. The "unholy three" went to work on a scheme to break free of their confines.

At 3:30 a.m. on Monday, March 12, Freng, Rogers and Burton made good on their plans after removing a portion of the iron lining to the jail's main corridor and digging through the south brick wall. The jail staff knew nothing of the caper until 1:30 p.m., giving the men a ten-hour head start, which they squandered. How did so much time pass before the escape was discovered? Jailer John Gertje explained that prisoners had the privilege of walking the corridor, as it had been lined with tool-proof boiler iron. However, the installation was less than complete. The plates were short, leaving a small portion of the wall uncovered at the top. A contractor installed a lighter material to the section of the wall, and the prisoners succeeded in loosening the bolts of the plating, exposing the brick wall behind it. After removing enough brick to create a one-foot-diameter hole, they exited the jail and slid down a drainage pipe from the roof. Getrje found no tools; the men had used their bare hands. So much for a secure jail. As strange as it may sound, the staff made a thorough examination of the jail only about three times a week. Obviously, no one supplied breakfast or lunch to Freng, Rogers and Burton that Monday.

The Nez Perce County Courthouse, showing the detached jail, circa 1915. *Courtesy of the Keith Vincent Collection.*

One has to question the memory of the sheriff's office. On August 13, 1901, five prisoners escaped from the jailhouse by cutting a hole eighteen inches square through the steel-lined wall by using a brace and bit provided from the outside by an accomplice. John Reamer, Frank Smith and Charles Smith were incarcerated for being cattle thieves. Charles Payne had been charged with burglary. The fifth, Max Mox, was just listed as "an Indian." Those escapees were never found.

Freng and Rogers made their way to Dry Gulch (near Asotin, Washington) to find a boat and prepared to meet their companion five miles downstream. Described as a "colored man," Burton remained in the city to find enough food for the group. Suspected of having a long criminal record, Burton had lived in Lewiston for about three years, running a hog ranch on Holbrook Island, but a black man in the city was pretty conspicuous in 1917. Officials found him beneath an abandoned building on C Street within hours of the escape. Freng and Rogers trusted him to bring supplies, but Burton was planning to take off on his own, concluding that he had a better chance of getting away without an unbalanced teenager and a bootlegger.

The search parties came up empty when it came to Freng and Rogers' whereabouts. Posses combed likely hiding places from Asotin to Alpowa, downstream from Lewiston. A horseman saw an individual hiding in a dry irrigation ditch, but no trace of that person was found. There were lots of footprints but no men.

After waiting in vain for several hours, Freng and Rogers decided that Freng should return to town to secure something to eat and meet Rogers downriver later that evening. Probably taking a route along the north bank of the Clearwater River until he reached the Eighteenth Street Bridge, he finally made his way to his parents' home between 3:00 and 4:00 a.m. Wednesday and picked up a few items of food. His father heard a noise, but as it did not reoccur, he thought it to be horses in a stable nearby. When the Frengs awoke that morning, Jewell's mother discovered that a loaf of bread was missing and the front door was open. Officials suspected that he remained hidden during the day among the brush along the river or in a vacant house.

Freng appeared at his parents' home around 6:00 p.m., intending to secure a supply of food, clothing and money to get him and Rogers out of the country. His parents promptly told him that he must return to the jail, an idea that he immediately opposed. Considered headstrong even as a boy, Jewell took a good deal of coaxing before he consented to return to the jail less than two blocks away. He would tell no one where Rogers was hiding. It would be only a matter of time, however. Ranches and settlements up and down the Snake River were alerted to the escapee. Without provisions, Rogers would need to surface sooner or later.

Freng would not find his new cell so accommodating. The jail had not considered using either of its two Pauly steel cells, which were escape proof. Too much faith had been placed in the plated walls.

A jury of local farmers from the Potlatch prairie region north of Lewiston was sworn in by Judge Scales on April 25, with the trial beginning two days later. Thirty witnesses, including five physicians, were served with subpoenas. The proceedings took less than three days. Freng's attorney, Clay McNamee, attempted to play the insanity card, termed "mental responsibility" in the testimony, but Freng's coldness and premeditation doomed that defense strategy. The jury returned a guilty verdict and a sentence of life in prison on May 1 after only an hour of deliberations. The jurors later revealed that, at first, the vote was six-to-six between a sentence of death or one for life imprisonment.

In an effort to distance herself from her Lewiston trauma, Anna Gifford traveled with baby Mary Virginia to Montana to visit her sisters, who lived in Valley Creek, near Arlee. There she met William "Ed" Schall, a widower with two young daughters. Ed and Anna were married in 1920, and she began to rebuild her life. As if Jewell's life had not already unraveled enough, his jailers did not expect what would happen next.

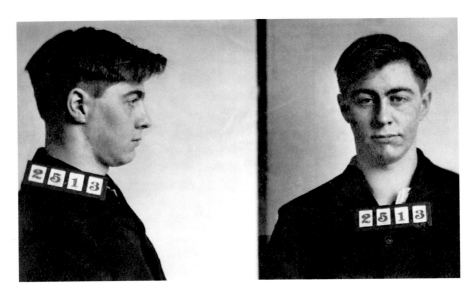

Jewell Richard Freng, 1917. *Courtesy of the Idaho State Historical Society, AR42 #2513.*

The draft for World War I found its way even into the cells of the state penitentiary. Jewell was duly registered on September 12, 1918, for possible duty. In 1920, he applied for a pardon. When Charles Gifford, Lester's father, learned of this, he dispatched local attorney Fred Butler to Boise, carrying many letters protesting any consideration of granting a pardon. The pardon board rejected Jewell's appeal on January 9, 1920. A life in prison without the hope of parole can do odd things to a person's mind.

On October 11, 1921, he visited the prison barbershop shortly after 8:00 a.m. When it came time for him to get a shave, he pulled a straight-edged razor from its package on the nearby counter before the barber could stop him. Holding his head down with one hand, he slashed his throat, severing both the jugular vein and carotid artery. He died within a minute, drenched in his own blood. The state shipped his body to Genesee, Idaho, where he was buried in the Genesee Valley Lutheran Cemetery. Both of his parents died in 1942 and were interred next to him.

The events of December 16, 1916, cast a very long shadow. Anna rarely spoke of that day and died on September 5, 1973, in Arlee. Nine decades later, the last principal in this tragedy, Mary Virginia Gifford Olson, died in Coeur d'Alene, Idaho, on February 19, 2007, leaving four generations of descendants. Only five weeks old the day her father was murdered, she was the last witness to a life cut off in a fit of irrational youthful animus.

3

A POTPOURRI OF PARANOIA, PERFIDY AND PUZZLING PREDICAMENTS

Once you begin being naughty, it is easier to go and on and on, and sooner or later something dreadful happens.
—*Laura Ingalls Wilder*

Some stories from Lewiston's shady past are just blips on the historical radar. They may have taken up a few column inches of space in the newspapers and then vanished from the collective memory. Nonetheless, the people and events do deserve retelling, if only to alert us to what can happen in any small city.

Convicted in 1924 of the murder of Lewiston police officer Gordon Harris, Darrel Thurston was sentenced to life imprisonment. The story took a strange turn once the jury began deliberating over what the sentence would be. The *Lewiston Morning Tribune* announced that it had an unnamed source said to be privy to the jury's discussions.

The newspaper had printed a story indicating that the jury would not accept a death penalty and inferred that a juror had lied in the preliminary selection phase of the trial. The trial judge cautioned the newspaper that jury deliberations were to remain secret, and hearsay should not be printed. Today, a mistrial would be declared for such a breach of conduct.

Thurston was incarcerated in the old state penitentiary, inmate 3440. He spent the rest of his life there, dying on July 20, 1942, of a heart ailment. Nicknamed "Scoop" for his abilities on the prison baseball team, he was a

Darrell Thurston, 1924. *Courtesy of the Idaho State Historical Society, AR42 #3440.*

popular inmate. Upon his death, fellow prisoners purchased a plot for him in Cloverdale Memorial Park.

Of the three men convicted in Harris' death, Thurston was the last one still in prison by 1935.

DONALD GOWER HAD RETURNED to duty with the Canadian army in August 1950, volunteering for service in the Korean War after serving as a commando in World War II. He was in training at Yakima, Washington, with the Second Field Regiment. "Looking for a peaceful place" to spend time while on Christmas leave, he came to Lewiston. On December 26, Gower stepped into the Victory Tavern at 314 Main Street (now Morgan's Alley). For some reason, another patron of the bar, Earl King, tried to provoke a fight with Gower, striking him. Gower refused to retaliate and left. King followed him to Eddie's Tavern, struck Gower again and insisted on taking it out into Main Street. What was King's problem?

As Gower tried to walk away down Main Street, King accosted him again. Things escalated very quickly. Attempting to elude King, Gower fell to the pavement. Seeing King approaching, Gower went into "automatic commando" and landed a well-placed punch that sent King down in a heap. Gower made sure he stayed down with a swift kick to King's head.

An ambulance was called, but King died en route to St. Joseph's Hospital. Gower was arrested and jailed for involuntary manslaughter. Bond was set at $1,500 ($15,000), which, of course, he did not have on him. So Gower spent the night in the city jail. He appealed to his commanding officer for "legal and moral counsel." Lieutenant William Coull, assistant quartermaster for the regiment, took custody of Gower on January 1, 1951, saying that Gower would be tried in Yakima, at Fort Lewis (near Tacoma, Washington) or in Canada. Surprisingly, none of that happen.

In early April 1951, Gower returned to the Nez Perce County Courthouse, where a court-martial was scheduled. Yes, that is correct. The Canadian army conducted a seven-officer court-martial in Lewiston, the first court-martial ever held in the city. Gower's attorney, Major D.H. Gillis, dismissed his client's kicking King in the head, saying, "A soldier is supposed to be instinctive, automatic." If Gower kicked King, he added, it "reflect[ed] training that the army regards as ideal."

Based on the autopsy report, Boise pathologist Dr. Joseph Beeman testified that King's death was the result of bleeding around the base of the brain. That injury could well have occurred as a result of King's head hitting the curbing on Main Street. About one hundred spectators crowded into the courtroom as the panel retired to deliberate. At 10:18 p.m., April 6, the verdict came back: not guilty. The audience cheered.

King had repeatedly picked a fight with the wrong guy. As Gower walked slowly from the courtroom, soldiers and civilians alike shook his hand. He had stood up to a bully and went back to army life.

TWENTY-FOUR-YEAR-OLD Lester Morlan went missing on August 27, 1948. He had told his wife he was going to Spokane, Washington, to look for work, but she then heard nothing from him. His wife begged Lewiston police to find him. Their daughters missed their father. The only foul play turned out to be of Lester's own making.

Convinced that his marriage was going to pieces, Lester wrote eight worthless checks between August 30 and September 10 worth $1,236 ($12,000). Money in hand, he headed for Portland, Oregon, where he was "stricken with remorse" and surrendered to police on September 26. His mother came from California and repaid the bad checks.

On October 16, he pleaded guilty to grand larceny in a Spokane court, which granted him three years' probation on the condition that he reimburse his mother. "The court intends to see that you do pay her back, as she has made a considerable sacrifice for you," warned Judge R.M. Webster.

Lester's wife was in the courtroom and told the judge she would stick by her husband. They would work to repair their marriage.

ON TUESDAY, FEBRUARY 11, 1947, Dorothy Drips disappeared. Employed at the *Lewiston Morning Tribune* as a linotype operator, Dorothy unexpectedly resigned on Monday evening. The next day, she was seen at a Lewiston bank withdrawing her savings. A fellow worker went to her apartment at 405 Second Avenue and found a note saying that she was going to commit suicide and where to find the money.

Her daughter hurried from Portland, Oregon, and told officials that she knew of no motive her mother would have had to take her own life. Dorothy's body was found in the Snake River by a railroad section foreman near Central Ferry, about sixty miles downstream from Lewiston, on April 25.

All of this sounds like a pretty clear case of suicide, but there is a wrinkle in the theory. When her body was found, her feet were tied together with an electric iron cord. There are no reports of the money being found.

YOU HAD TO BE CAREFUL when visiting Lewiston in the old days. Charles Bates—chief of detectives for the Butte, Montana police department—learned the hard way on October 13, 1908. He was in town on the hunt for a thief wanted in Butte and stayed at the Raymond House (*Hidden History* 104). His travel budget must have been pretty meager, for Bates was using a cot on that Tuesday night.

He was sleeping serenely with his pistol in his hand when a thief, who had no respect for detectives, relieved Bates of his wallet, which contained $8 ($210). The detective later made light of the event but ensured that it did not happen again. He knew that he would be "guyed" (held up to ridicule) by members of the Butte force upon his return to Butte. A plainclothes officer, Bates thought he knew all the methods of the county and agricultural fair crooks in the Northwest. The Lewiston-Clarkston Fair was in full swing at the time, and petty thieves followed the circuit of festivals looking for easy marks. It turns out that Bates was one of them.

BURGLARY IS SUPPOSED TO be a silent crime committed with stealth. In 1897, Thomas Clark did not get that memo. On May 6, Clark broke into a house occupied by a wealthy local Chinese vegetable farmer. The workmen on the property discovered the intruder just as he found a money cache in a bed and was shaking the silver pieces onto the floor—so much for a quiet crime and getaway.

The "Mongolian workmen" reacted to the noise and held up Clark by brandishing garden tools as weapons. A messenger was sent to a nearby telephone to call the sheriff. Clark offered a bribe to his captors, but they flatly refused. The sheriff found Clark meekly awaiting the authorities, who held him for burglary in the second degree.

KIDS LOVE TO DIG IN the dirt. It's what they sometimes find that gets people excited.

Late in the afternoon of February 4, 1904, a small boy was playing in a ravine near the eastern city limits, which, at the time, were at Twentieth Street. The lad saw a bone sticking out of the bank. When he extracted it, he found it to be a man's leg. The owner of the property was notified, along with the police. After additional digging, an entire skeleton was unearthed.

News of the find created a good deal of excitement in town, and many people visited the site in the next few hours. Chief Abbott Masters, after examining the bones, declared that they were those of an Indian who had probably been buried there about twenty years before, when the neighborhood was not inside the city limits.

At about 5:00 p.m. on January 15, 1906, children were playing in a lot in their neighborhood when Charley Lee went running home to excitedly tell Mrs. V.A. Bilderback that her dog was playing with a human hand. Police confirmed the finding after a brief investigation. Dr. Costello said it was the limb of an old woman. The gruesome discovery was made near a pavilion that was used in the summer for dancing. An arm was also found. Police tied up the dog and denied it food for most of a day in hopes that the animal might lead them to the rest of the remains. No one was reported missing in the area. The case was never solved. The dance pavilion in question may well have been the site were a small park called Dreamland was later established, located where Main and D Streets converge at Eleventh (*Hidden History* 106).

Human bones, bits of clothing and an outdated union button were found on August 17, 1961, in a burned-over area on the Lewiston Hill by two teenagers who had discovered a skull the previous day in the brush-covered slide area. The unidentified person may have been buried in a shallow grave.

The skeleton, complete except for toe and finger bones, was reconstructed in the front yard of Jim Yeoman at 822 Warner Avenue. He and two friends had been on a hike when they came upon the skull about three-quarters of the distance up from the Snake River to the top of the hill. They returned with another friend the next day and found a pelvis and two leg bones on the top of the ground. Digging a shallow trench at the site produced ribs, two arm bones and the spine.

The position of the skeleton showed that the person was lying on his back at the time of death. Rotten pieces of what appeared to be heavy clothing and the heel of a hiking shoe were nearby. The union button bore the name of the International Woodworkers of America, which was affiliated with the Congress of Industrial Organizations (CIO). The CIO merged with the American Federation of Labor in 1956, so the remains would have been lying there for at least five years.

"The bones were in the only brushy spot on the hillside," Yeoman said. "We couldn't tell if the body had been buried, or rocks had slid over it." The police department took custody of the remains and called in a pathologist to make a determination. Interestingly, a dog skeleton was found with the body.

IN APRIL 1941, ROBERT "Frenchy" Bech (aka Robert Beck or William Carder) was released from Idaho State Penitentiary after serving one year and two months for a first-degree burglary conviction in Kootenai County. He came to Lewiston and found a job working for the Hepton ranch on Lindsay Creek Road, just east of the city. His bosses described

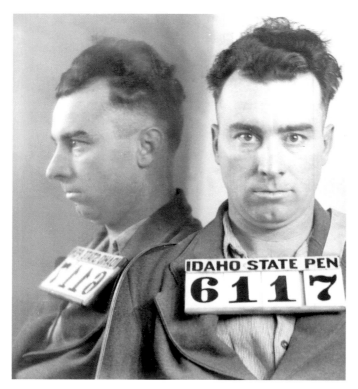

Robert Bech, 1940. *Courtesy of the Idaho State Historical Society, AR42 #6117.*

Robert as a "perfect" employee and a gentleman during the months of his employment.

As time passed, he began to fixate on Lillian Boxleitner, another worker at the ranch, but never gave any hint of his feelings. He had asked her to go to a movie with him, but she had refused. Most people thought the matter closed. It wasn't. Lillian did not know the extent of his grim love for her.

On Sunday, November 2, Robert was waiting for her at the ranch when she returned after an outing with a friend, Elmer Pazer. Robert had an old-fashioned double-barreled shotgun. A quarrel ensued. Frightened, Lillian began to run in one direction and Elmer in the other. Robert fired first on Pazer, wounding him slightly when the full force of the blast was deflected by an old wood stove. Robert turned his attention back to Lillian, chasing her down about one hundred yards from the farmhouse, where he killed her. Reloading the old gun, he turned it on himself.

Robert left a three-hundred-word letter addressed to the county sheriff. In the letter, he explained his thinking:

> *I am killing Lillian Boxleitner because I love her more than anything else in this world. I hereby ask God to forgive me for what I am going to do to her.*

In a footnote to his explanation, investigators found a hastily penned will in which Bech left his back wages to John Moore, a Clarkston High School student, whom Bech called "my only friend outside of Mrs. Hepton."

THE ADVENTIST SABBATH CHURCH held a special memorial service on April 1, 1964, for young man in the congregation who had been robbed and stabbed nine times by a mugger on March 23 in Mount Morris, a section of the Bronx. What makes this story so special is that the Advent Sabbath Church is in Harlem, New York, and the young man was a blond, blue-eyed, twenty-nine-year-old man who had lived in Lewiston.

David Watts came to Lewiston in 1955 to join his sister and grandfather and was employed for part of that time by the local Western Union office and delivered telegrams on a bicycle around town. He left in 1958 to join the army and settled in New York after his discharge.

Watts loved Harlem and was the only white member of the congregation. Reverend Thomas Hughes gave the eulogy:

> *We didn't expect him to live in Harlem. But we discovered he was not a fraud. He was without guile.* [David] *did more for integration as an*

individual than we have done as a people, because he lived with us. He got along well with Negro children and took some to the movies and sat on curbstones telling them Bible stories. He went about Harlem like a missionary, doing Bible studies and talking to people, melting antagonism and hatred.

Watts lived in a rook in the heart of Harlem for seven years, working the last two years as porter for fifty dollars a week and as an errand boy to support his Seventh-Day Adventist ministry. So many people wanted to attend the funeral service that the event had to be moved to the United Sabbath Adventist Church.

David's family did not have the money to reclaim his body. Reverend Hughes concluded by saying, "Dave belonged to us. It's only right that we bury him."

ON SEVERAL OCCASIONS, Lewiston's city officials have not been averse to a little abuse of power. A case in point occurred in December 1903. The residents of Normal Hill eagerly awaited the installation of a sewer system to replace the cesspools that befouled the air of the new neighborhoods. At its December 11 meeting, the city council became embroiled in a "hot discussion" over the recent visit of Spokane, Washington's city engineer to examine the work being done on the new project.

Cassius Colby revealed that he had learned that fellow councilman Leon LeQuime (*Lost Lewiston* 33) had, when the sewer projects bids were let, approached the firm of Naylor and Norlin with a proposition. If the contractors would withdraw from the competition, they would receive $1,000 ($26,000) from each of the fourteen other firms competing for the contract. If Naylor and Norlin wished to remain candidates, they could pay each of the other bidders $1,000 and then jack up their original bid by $28,000 ($730,000).

LeQuime interrupted Colby, saying that Colby was a "damned liar," and dared Colby to sign his name to the charges. Colby said that he was perfectly willing to sign such a statement and asserted that he would publicize why LeQuime so actively complained about Naylor and Norlin.

Colby yielded the floor and sat down. LeQuime had nothing more to say and later refused to make any statement on the matter. The charge of attempted bribery was confirmed by N.C. Naylor, a senior member of the company, who stated that he had witnesses to testify that LeQuime had approached him with the bribe. LeQuime resigned from the city council in disgrace but went on to serve as a governing board member of the Lewiston Commercial Club (now the chamber of commerce) and the district manager of the Continental Oil Company. His April 16, 1935 obituary states that he was a "former member of the city council" but makes no mention of the bribery scandal that led to his resignation.

THE IDAHO INDUSTRIAL ACCIDENT BOARD meeting in Lewiston on July 22, 1937, was a little unusual. A hearing was held to determine which of two women was the lawful widow of Edward C. Rose, a pilot who had been killed in a May 1936 accident near St. Anthony, Idaho. Who would get his accident insurance payout?

Ruby Rose, who lived in Clarkston at the time, claimed she had married Rose in Idaho Falls in December 1935. Anna Marie King declared that she had married Edward in Phoenix, Arizona, in November 1928, when he identified himself as "Monte King." Edward came to Lewiston in 1931 and had been active in the local aviation community, boasting that he had flown in the Mexican Revolution. Newspapers did not report the final decision. Family historians located his personal scrapbook from the 1920s and discovered the story of a man who was desperately trying to reinvent himself.

WHILE WE ARE ON THE subject of marriage: divorce cases rarely reach the hearing of a state supreme court, but on June 22, 1915, a nasty Lewiston marital dispute did just that.

Harry Gilbert Darwin was an 1887 engineering graduate of Columbia University and rose to be first deputy commissioner of the Tenement House Department of New York before coming to Idaho in 1908, when he became the vice-president and general manager of the Waha-Lewiston Land and Water Company. Widowed in 1891, he had remarried and was living with his second wife, Edythe, and Gilbert, his child from his first marriage. By 1910, the marriage was, to say the least, rocky. Edythe had become violent and left the home for Spokane. In affidavits filed with the court, she was described as treating her husband "in a cruel and inhumane manner, rendering his life burdensome and inflicting grievous bodily injury and grievous mental suffering, anguish and pain." On one occasion, she reportedly tried to kill him.

Harry was forced to commit Edythe to the Crystal Springs Sanitarium in Portland, Oregon, for three months that year. Harry stayed with Mrs. Norman Buck during these episodes (*Historic Firsts* 81). In one account dating from the spring of 1913, she reportedly "ridiculed and derided the people of Lewiston, and used profane and vulgar language on many occasions in the hearing of their minor child." Edythe drank heavily, "indulging herself excessively…exhibiting herself upon the streets and in houses in Lewiston and Clarkston, Wash."

Harry obtained a default divorce in 1914, but Edythe appealed to the Idaho Supreme Court, contending that her side of the story had not been adequately represented, although she had responded. She argued that, because of her mental state, she was actually incapable of responding to the numerous summonses. The court disagreed in a split decision.

IVOR AND DOLLIE CARROLL moved to the Lewiston Orchards in 1924 from Ohio and operated a truck farm. On Saturday, January 10, 1931, Dollie escaped from her own Lewiston Orchards home, but not to flee from fire or an infestation of mice. Her husband, Ivor, had suddenly snapped and

Ivor and Dollie Carroll, 1917. Their son, Ardra, died on November 25. *Courtesy of Vivian Rowlette.*

"Old Robber's Roost," east of the city near Lindsay Creek, showing "Lookout Point," circa 1930. An Allen & Thurber single-shot boot pistol was found in a cave located high up in the ravine. The cave was likely a "shebang," or hideout. *Courtesy of the Nez Perce County Historical Society.*

had kept his wife and their three children captive in their house for two and a half days. He threatened them with an axe, a gun and fire during their imprisonment. Police officers found an open can of gasoline in the home. Ivor threatened to toss a match in the gasoline, setting the house on fire and burning the trapped family.

Sheriff Harry Dent and a deputy rushed to the home after being contacted by Dollie, who had to leave her three sons with Ivor when she made her escape. The officers spent an hour negotiating with him before gaining entrance to the house and taking Ivor into custody. He was committed to the North Idaho Insane Asylum at Orofino. The family was reunited after Ivor responded to treatment for a transient psychotic episode. He died in 1954. Dollie passed away in 1965.

GEORGE SHOAF WAS A WRITER for the Socialist weekly *Appeal to Reason* and had been dispatched to Los Angeles, California, to investigate the explosion that wrecked the offices of the *Los Angeles Times* and killed twenty-one men on August 1, 1910. In a letter published in August 1911, Shoaf stated that he had gathered information that would "create consternation from coast to coast" and charge full responsibility for the explosion to Harrison Gray Otis, the owner of the *Times*.

That week, Shoaf went missing. The *Appeal* claimed that he "was either kidnapped or possibly murdered." Police learned that scuffling had been heard in his room in a Los Angeles boardinghouse. His crushed hat and a pipe filled with lead were found in his room the next morning. There was one problem: it was a hoax. He had no proof against Otis. The provocateurs under arrest for the bombing were indeed the culprits. In truth, Shoaf was hiding from an angry Lewiston father.

George Shoaf, 1912. *From* Common Cause.

Ernest Untermann had come to Idaho as a correspondent to cover the 1907 trial of Bill Haywood for his role in the assassination of former Idaho governor Frank Steunenberg. In 1910, he ran as the Socialist candidate for the office of governor. In the fall of 1911, he was living in Lewiston and was concerned about the welfare of his daughter Elsa, whom he could not locate. Untermann wrote to Eugene Debs, the Socialist Party leader, and called for his assistance.

Not long after Shoaf's disappearance, Piet Vlag, the editor of a competing Socialist newspaper, intercepted a letter from Shoaf to seventeen-year-old Elsa, who was obviously his mistress. Vlag instructed Elsa to remain mum on Shoaf's whereabouts and her own while Vlad tried to extort money from the Socialist Party to keep the letter from coming to light. Vlad sent Elsa to Holland. When she got the opportunity to explain her part of the story, she wrote:

> *Last winter when I first began to live with* [Shoaf], *I told him that we would have to be nothing more than brother and sister, that I could never love him. But he was so miserable, and made so many appeals to me that I could not hold out against him…I know things perfectly heinous that he has done in his work, things that he loathed…If I cannot love him for what he is, I will love him for what he might have been.*

Untermann's appeal to Debs soon dissolved into a shouting match by letter. He had warned Debs in 1907 about Shoaf, who had been charged with the statutory rape of a fifteen-year-old girl. Untermann gave Debs an ultimatum, and Debs chose to back Fred Warren, the editor of his own magazine, rather than get involved. In Debs' opinion, the affair between George and Elsa was a private one. A careful reading of the correspondence indicates that Warren knew that Bill Haywood was indeed guilty as charged in the murder of Steunenberg. Untermann had uncovered an "inconvenient truth."

In his "post-radical" years, Untermann became a famed illustrator known for his images of dinosaurs.

POLICE CHIEF ABBOTT MASTERS came close to being the first fatality among those who have served in Lewiston's law enforcement department.

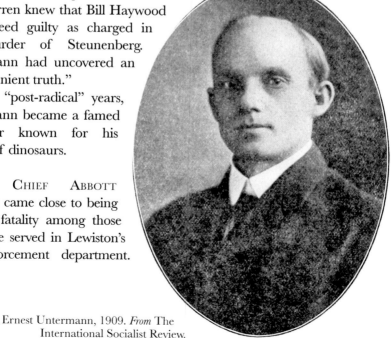

Ernest Untermann, 1909. *From* The International Socialist Review.

On September 26, 1904, he narrowly escaped being stabbed to death while arresting a drunken man who was "making himself generally obnoxious by loud talking and swearing." Too inebriated to give his name, the man was a stranger to locals, who thought him to be a road bum.

Masters noticed the drunk walking up and down Main Street and told him to get out of sight or he would be arrested. The man swore at Masters and sneaked into a saloon. It did not take long before the sot was back out haranguing people. Again, Masters ordered him off the street, but this time, the man became abusive. The chief grabbed him by the arm and started to pull it behind the man's back.

"I'll stop you right here," shouted the bum as he proceeded to pull out a large pocketknife concealed in his coat. He slashed at Masters, coming within inches of his stomach. The two men struggled. Two more attempts were made to stab Masters, who finally gained control and forced his assailant to drop the knife. You would think that a charge of assault with the deadly weapon would have been in order. No, the chief let him off with a fine for being drunk and disorderly. Drunken men who could not pay their fines got street cleaning duty.

Lewiston has had a long history of using prisoners for public projects. On January 4, 1875, the city council decided to put prisoners to work cleaning Lewiston's unpaved streets. The council reaffirmed its decision on August 14, 1899. The practice of using "convict labor" continues to this day for special projects, such as the Fifth Street steps, Vollmer Bowl and summer renovations in the schools.

ON JANUARY 25, 1905, Tung Lee, a Chinese merchant in Lewiston, was arrested and charged with sending an obscene picture through the mail to Myrtle Burlington, a local resident. Lee posted a $200 ($5,200) bond.

Lee admitted to having had the picture in question, but he claimed that Myrtle came to his store frequently and when he showed her the picture, she asked for it. He complied with her request. He further asserted that Myrtle had been ill and that he had given her $5 ($130). She had asked for money again, but he refused. After that, she came back to his store and asked him to write her name and address on an envelope. Are we talking about a set up here?

4

A SUSPICIOUS CASE OF SELF-DELIVERANCE

Any truth is better than indefinite doubt.
—*Arthur Conan Doyle,* The Adventure of the Yellow Face

Almost any story is some kind of lie.
—*Orson Wells*

In early February 1903, city engineer Edson Briggs and his team of surveyors discovered a relic of old Lewiston on a hillside while working on an extension of Lewiston's waterworks reservoir, about one mile southeast of town. The object was a marble slab with an inscription:

Lodowick C. Fitch

Born in West Bloomingdale, New York
January 2, 1827

Died at Lewiston, I.T.
January 27, 1864

Few Lewiston old-timers had any memories of a local businessman whose body was buried so long before. Those recollections were badly worn with the years, as the headstone itself would attest.

Lodowick Champlin Fitch Jr., or "L.C." to his associates, was the scion of a wealthy and well-established West Bloomfield, New York merchant family. His father, Lodowick Sr., was "extensively known in the western part of this state for his rare business and social qualities." Born in February 1788, he served as an original director of the Ontario and Livingstone Mutual Insurance Company, was a leading figure of the Whig Party in New York and worked as a local attorney. He married Sarah Dean on September 17, 1822. Sarah also brought an impressive pedigree to the marriage, as she was the daughter of Stewart Dean, captain of the armed sloop *Beaver* in the Revolutionary War.

The Fitches raised nine children in their West Bloomfield home—sons Stewart, Lodowick Jr. and Elisha, along with their six daughters. By 1850, all but two of the children had left home. Elisha went to sea and quickly rose to be the master of various United States mail steamers, notably the *Washington*. Lodowick Sr. died on April 20, 1854. Elisha had much on his mind when he left New York for Southampton, England, a few days later.

On May 2, he came across the packet ship *Winchester*, which had been de-masted in a major gale, causing the ship to go adrift with 482 passengers and crew aboard. Maneuvering the *Washington* as close as he dared, Elisha dispatched his first officer and four volunteers to board the *Winchester*. Their boat began to sink as they reached the ship, but the rescue team was "snatched from a watery grave," as the *Sabbath Recorder* reported.

Elisha directed lifeboats into position, and the last survivors left the ship only minutes before it sank from sight. Several persons had died in the storm, and the crew had laid them out on the rolling deck. Remaining to be the last persons off the wreck, the *Washington*'s first officer P.W. King and the captain of the *Winchester* made one final survey of the dead and found a woman who was still breathing. For their heroism, Elisha and his crew were awarded medals and large monetary rewards and were repeatedly fêted in New York City.

Elisha went on to command the steamship *Sonora*, carrying passengers from New York to Bremen, Germany, and died at sea aboard the ship on July 22, 1858, leaving his wife, Louisa, with four children in Brooklyn. However, where was Lodowick Jr. in this story?

His name appears for the first time in the March 22, 1854 edition of the *Sacramento (CA) Daily Union*. He had left Panama earlier that month aboard the SS *California*, bound for San Francisco, which he reached on March 21, one month before his father's death. It would be many more months before he would hear the news of his father's burial and years before he would read of the drama aboard the *Winchester*.

Daily Alta California, June 12, 1861. An advertisement placed by L.C. Fitch appears in the center column. *Courtesy of the California Digital Newspaper Collection, University of California, Riverside.*

His life in California is a patchwork of isolated facts. At least one unconfirmed source reports that he married in 1855. What we know of his work comes from the 1861 edition of the *Langley San Francisco City Directory*, in which he is listed as the agent for the McCarthy Automatic Steam Boiler Safety Valve. He arrived back in New York aboard the steamship *North Star* from Aspinwall, Panama, in May 1860, to negotiate his contract with McCarthy. Business took him to Louisiana in December, where he is found checking into the St. Charles Hotel in New Orleans on the thirteenth. His stay in the East lasted until February 1861, when he finally embarked for his return to San Francisco via Panama. The April 8 issue of the *Daily Alta California* reported on the recent return of "Mr. S. Fitch" and included an extensive description of the safety valve. The man in question was Samuel S. Fitch. A new market for the steam valve seemed ready at hand, and Lodowick wasted no time demonstrating the new technology. Then, the lure of Idaho began to call our enterprising thirty-five-year-old.

Fitch & Company, 1862. *Courtesy of Special Collections and Archives, University of Idaho Library, 5-007-4a.*

By August 1862, the firm of Fitch & Company, a dry goods and general merchandise business, was a fixture on the corner of Third and D Streets in Lewiston, where the city's community development offices are now located. Based on the best evidence, at some point in 1863, Fitch took on a junior partner, Levin Bacon, a young man with an obvious future. Bacon was the only Democratic member of the First Idaho Territorial Legislature that convened in Lewiston on December 7, 1863. He was soon swept up in the events surrounding the brutal murders of Lloyd Magruder and his companions in October of that year.

In August 1940, William Bacon, Levin's son, visited Lewiston. He related to a reporter that his father was the hangman at the March 4, 1864 execution of the killers (*Historic Firsts* 47–48). His father spoke often of the events that transpired at the foot of Poe Grade (Thirteenth Street) that fateful Friday morning. Levin was an acquaintance of one of the convicted men and felt bad about the role he was about to play in his death. However, the condemned criminal turned to him and said, "Go ahead. Somebody has to do it."

Lewiston must have been a dismal place in 1864. The census that year listed only 225 inhabitants, many of them newly arrived Chinese. The town's very existence seemed threatened by its dwindling numbers and by reports of a possible withdrawal of federal troops from nearby Fort Lapwai. On March 1, Fitch wrote to Brigadier General Benjamin Alvord, commander of the U.S. Volunteers in the Oregon District. In his letter, Fitch told Alvord, "So far as I can judge the public verdict of the people is that the establishment of Fort Lapwai prevented an Indian war." In his reply on March 14, Alvord assured him that any rumors of an abandonment of the fort were unfounded and included a compliment: "It gratifies me to hear such language from an intelligent source, as my efforts for the defense of Idaho Territory have been underrated in some quarters." The fort was going to stay. Fitch had a lot invested in Lewiston.

On April 4, 1864, Nez Perce County held its first regularly scheduled election to fill public offices. Bacon won the position as the first elected Nez Perce County assessor in the balloting that secured the office of county superintendent of schools for Lodowick Fitch. The next mention of Fitch appears in the October 15, 1864 edition of the *Daily Union*. And the news was not good.

> *SUICIDE.—We learn from the* Golden Age, *of Lewiston (I.T.), that L.C. Fitch, a respectable hardware merchant of that city, committed suicide on Thursday, September 22ᵈ, by shooting himself with a revolver, the ball entering the right side of the head, near the ear, coming out of the left side, just above the temple. The deceased was conducting a lucrative business, of perfectly sane mind, enjoying the confidence and respect of the community.*

When Briggs and his staff located the grave and headstone more than thirty-eight years later, the Fitch name meant nothing to them. The surveyors were not surprised by the discovery, as several isolated grave sites have been found in or near the city. A reporter for the *Lewiston Morning Tribune* queried "some of the older residents of Lewiston," who stated that Fitch had committed suicide and "at his request was buried in the lonely spot where his grave was found."

Those are the facts accepted at the time. However, let us explore Lodowick's death using the methods employed by modern law enforcement investigators in cases of suicide and attempt to answer whether Fitch took his own life or someone murdered him.

In his work *Practical Homicide Investigation: Tactics, Procedures, and Forensic Techniques*, Vernon Geberth, a forty-year veteran of the Bronx Police Department and commander of its homicide task force, outlines three basic considerations to establish that a death is really a suicide:

> *1. The presence of the weapon or means of death at the scene*
> *2. Injuries or wounds that are obviously self-inflicted, or could have been inflicted by the deceased*

3. The existence of a motive or intent on the part of the victim to take his or her own life

All right all you *CSI* fans, what conclusions can we reach based on the scanty evidence?

First, the report from the *Golden Age* states that a revolver delivered the fatal wound. If the revolver was still at the scene, a reasonable person would ask, "Was it his revolver?" Did those who found his body just assume that a revolver was used?

Second, while it is true that the wound described in the *Golden Age* could have been inflicted by Fitch, whoever reported finding the body would not likely have had the skills necessary to distinguish the beveling of the bones of the skull found at entry and exit points. Fired at the angle described in the news report, the bullet would have produced very similar damage to his head. Was Fitch right-handed? If he had been shot at very close range, any revolver of that period would have deposited considerable stippling, the soot residue left by a gunshot at close range and not blocked by clothing. No one mentioned powder burns.

You are probably asking where was the county coroner? The first documented election of a Nez Perce County coroner took place in November 1872, when Walter Dyer won the office. Dyer had come to the county in 1862 and was a longtime member of the farming department at the Nez Perce Reservation. Thus, we are left with unqualified people making unqualified claims.

Before continuing to a discussion of motive, the location of Fitch's body, the timing of the report and the headstone raise some troubling questions. His grave was found near what is now Twenty-sixth Street in Lewiston. At the time, the site was about two miles from the center of town, too far for the direction of a gunshot to be determined, and few people were startled to hear gunshots in Lewiston in September 1864. As no road ran near the site, an innocent passerby would have come across his body only by accident. If Fitch did leave a note, he would have had no idea how long it would be before someone found his remains.

The headstone certainly raises questions, as the inscription contains glaring discrepancies. The headstone gives his hometown as West Bloomingdale, New York, with a birth date of January 2. Fitch was born on January 3 in West Bloomfield. Well, it is at least close. Most surprising, however, is the difference in the day of death. The stone reads January 27, when the reported date was September 22. Unless Fitch ordered his own stone and then delayed his suicide, someone with a faulty memory had the marker carved at a much later date. We do know at least one thing about the stone: it was carved before July 1, 1890, when Idaho gained statehood. Fitch's grave remained untended and undocumented for nearly four decades.

So then, what would have been Fitch's motive to kill himself? The *Golden Age* report stated that he enjoyed "the confidence and respect of the community." He was entrusted with the management of the school system, and Lewiston has always taken its schools and those who lead them very seriously.

Financial insecurities do not prove to be a reasonable answer. His hardware company was "a lucrative business." Indeed, business registries and newspapers continued to mention "Fitch & Co" at its Third and D Streets location as late as 1866. The same old-timers who remembered Fitch did so as a partner of "Fitch & Bacon," a name that does not appear in any primary sources and would lead us to believe that Bacon assumed ownership after Lodowick's death. Yes, I know. I too am asking who would have benefited from his death.

One might speculate that depression may have been a factor. Research has demonstrated that four out of five men who kill themselves (usually by gunshot) resort to self-deliverance as a result of depression. In *Men and Depression*, James Ellison notes some important issues:

> *Women who are depressed often cry and talk about the sadness, low energy and loss of fun. A depressed man may not want anyone to see him as weak or out of control. His depression takes a different form. He may show a bad temper or even anger instead of sadness. He might have trouble working. He might blame a physical problem such as arthritis for pain that is more than you would expect with that disease. He might get into alcohol or drugs, or unsafe behavior. Men are less likely to ask for help.*

If Lodowick Fitch suffered from depression, no one recognized it or probably would have. He was, to everyone, a man "of perfectly sane mind." No one saw any loss of interest in his work or an inability to concentrate on the details and responsibilities of his business—both of which are key signs and symptoms of depression in men. Marital strife can also be discounted. A thorough search of the California marriage records and New York genealogical charts fails to show any union, and the report of his death makes no reference to a widow.

We finally come to a crucial piece of evidence: the "suicide note," which would be an indication of intent. Fitch had supposedly left instructions to bury him where he was found. Such a note would suggest suicide. However, the idea of a note of burial instructions arose only in 1903, and death notes are left in less than 25 percent of all cases. Let's assume for a moment that a note was found. Today, investigators are schooled to treat suicide notes like any other piece of crime scene evidence. They will study many features: handwriting, angle on the page, slant of the letters and the spacing of the words. More importantly, an exemplar, or sample, of the victim's handwriting will be compared to the note. That most certainly did not happen in September 1864.

Whoever found his body took the note at face value. As that scrap of paper was long ago discarded, we cannot compare it with the characteristics of the genuine and the fake. A murderer could have penned the note or had Fitch write it before killing him. One has to wonder why Fitch left no instructions describing how his company was to be managed. "Bury me here" leaves a lot to the imagination.

Levin Bacon continued to live in Lewiston after Fitch's death. If anyone suspected him, they were not talking. It was not the first or last time that a felon would live undisturbed in Lewiston. He hired on as a driver for Felix Warren by 1869. In 1871, he and two friends won a parcel of land on Tenth Street in a poker game and subsequently quitclaimed it as the site for a new

Benjamin Alvord, circa 1866. *Courtesy of the Library of Congress.*

public school. On June 15, 1876, we find him in St. George, Utah, where he married eighteen-year-old Cecelia White, an English immigrant twenty years his junior. The Bacons moved to Dry Canyon, Utah, and started a family, which included two sons and a daughter. On January 26, 1892, Levin suffered disfiguring injuries to his face, hands and body when a spark from his candle ignited a box of blasting caps. He did not fully recover and died in June 1896.

Benjamin Alvord would have more to say about Lewiston five months after Lodowick's death. Governor Caleb Lyon had fled the territory and an arrest warrant after the second territorial legislature voted to move the capital to Boise City. A local judge placed his interim secretary under house arrest and locked the territorial seal and essential government documents in the prison. President Lincoln's patience with the chaos ran out, and he ordered Alvord to settle the matter, which he did, directing a detachment of the First Oregon Volunteer Cavalry from Lapwai to accompany Clinton DeWitt Smith, the new secretary, to seize the emblems of office. The deed was done on March 30, 1865, and north Idaho residents have never stopped talking about it.

The discovery of Fitch's grave site in 1903 moved his sisters, Annie and Mary, to have his remains exhumed and transported, along with the headstone, to Pontiac, Michigan, where the sisters lived for decades. Lodowick's mother, Sarah, had remarried and then died there in October 1878, knowing her son was dead without being able to find his grave.

Fitch was reburied in Oak Hill Cemetery, his inscription being added to Sarah's monument. The timing of this familial and

Relocated Fitch headstone. *Courtesy of Oak Hill Cemetery, Pontiac, Michigan.*

final act of love is confirmed by a simple fact: Lewiston is referred to as being in Idaho, not the Idaho Territory. A Michigan engraver would have had no reason to etch "Idaho Territory" into the granite monolith in 1903.

Winston Churchill once described the Soviet Union as "a riddle, wrapped in a mystery, inside an enigma." The death of Lodowick Champlin Fitch Jr. is no less a conundrum.

HUMANS HAVE BEEN USING hallucinogens since ancient times. As early as 3400 BCE, opium poppies, called the "joy plant," were cultivated in Mesopotamia. Alexander the Great may have introduced the substance into Persia and India. People will try just about anything for a high. In October 1916, John Kelley, an aged Lewiston laborer, was committed to the county jail by Judge George Erb to await examination on a charge of insanity.

It seems that Kelley was using Jamaica ginger to such an extent that his mental ability and nervous system were completely wrecked. Jamaica ginger (also called "Jake" because of the limp many users developed) was a popular, cheap and highly alcoholic drink. Producers added triorthocresyl phosphate (TOCP) to the formula to fool federal tests. A "patent medicine," the government forced manufacturers to add ginger to make the drink so bitter that no one would want to drink it. That did not work.

The problem was that TOCP is a slow-acting neurotoxin that first creates muscular weakness in the arms and legs. Some users became so impaired that they claimed to have had a stroke. During Prohibition, Jamaica ginger produced hundreds of cases of paralysis.

The source of Kelley's supply can only be guessed at, given the scores of bars, saloons and brothels that served any and all sorts of libations.

5

THE MAN WITH A TWISTED FOOT

Passion is a positive obsession. Obsession is a negative passion.
—Paul Carvel

The *Los Angeles Herald's* June 26, 1909 issue featured a front page announcing that Robert Peary was thought to have reached the North Pole. That world-famous event paled in comparison with another story that ran just two columns to its right. Searchers had located the crab-eaten body of a woman whose life had traveled a path from literal rags to riches, and the path led back to Lewiston.

In the spring of 1886, seventeen-year-old Zettella Roup realized she was pregnant. It was not a happy discovery; she was not married. Nearing the time of delivery and not knowing if she could care for a child as an unwed mother, Zettella persuaded Ralph Sturtevant—the Asotin County, Washington prosecuting attorney—to protect the child, who would be a girl born on November 30. Shortly thereafter, Zettella married Matthew Witz, who gave the baby his name—Anna Pearl Witz. This girl's death more than two decades later would stun the country, filling newspapers in countless towns and cities with lurid tales.

In November 1887, Anna's stepfather, Matthew, and Henry Grayson, his employer, were at loggerheads over back pay resulting from a mining project. Grayson ambushed Matthew and killed him with a shotgun blast. In March 1888, Grayson escaped from the Asotin jail by cutting through a wall. He was recaptured and put on trial. His brother, a wealthy San Francisco mining executive, spent more than $10,000 ($260,000) to ensure his acquittal.

Zettella and Anna came to Lewiston after Matthew's murder, but a widow with a child found it difficult to find employment amid so much notoriety. Life prospects were bleak. Prostitution was not an option, and no marriage proposals were in sight. So mother and daughter pulled up stakes and moved to Minnesota, where Zettella met and married Albert Kight on July 19, 1889. The newlyweds found that they could not properly care for Anna Pearl.

After a short stay with relatives in Kansas City, Anna came back to Minneapolis and was soon in the care of a streetcar driver named Green and his wife, who were more than willing to allow someone else raise her if they could provide a home better than the Greens could afford. And so it was that the family of Charles and Laura Thompson came into Anna's life. A veteran of the Civil War, serving for nearly three years with the First Minnesota Infantry, Charles owned a profitable harness-making business and was known to most people as "Colonel." Engaged in charitable work with the Associated Charities of Minneapolis, Laura learned of Anna Pearl's situation and quickly grew attached to the brown-eyed, golden-haired child. The Thompsons adopted her on October 13, 1890, and changed her name to Edith May. Soon her life would be a universe away from those lean and humble days in Lewiston.

Edith became the delight of the Thompsons' social circle. When she reached the age of eight, her parents discovered her gift for music, singing in particular. Voice lessons seemed out-of-reach for the modest income that Charles was earning, but Edith's prospects took an unexpected turn. Lyman Gage, secretary of the treasury in the McKinley administration, counted Laura Thompson among his Minneapolis friends and was an occasional visitor at the Thompson's new residence on the shore of Chesapeake Bay near McDaniel, Maryland. Lyman became "Papa Gage" to Edith and would be so closely identified with her subsequent education that many people thought him to be her guardian.

Both Gage and Maryland governor Frank Brown recognized Edith's musical talent. Brown begged the Thompsons to allow him to have her trained for the stage. Young girls from important families did not do that in those days. When Lloyd Lowndes succeeded Brown as governor, he too added his vote to the plan to have Edith trained as a vocalist and instrumentalist, which occurred at the Peabody Conservatory of Music and the LeFebvre School of Music, both in Baltimore.

During the course of her studies, she frequently visited the White House and entertained William and Ida McKinley, who would often seat her between them as they took their daily afternoon carriage ride down Pennsylvania Avenue. When Edith was fifteen, Gage persuaded Laura to

Lyman Gage, circa 1899. *Courtesy of the Bureau of Engraving and Printing.*

accompany Edith to Paris, at his expense, to continue her musical studies. Edith counted Frank Vanderlip, the moving force behind the Federal Reserve System, among her closest friends.

An unconfirmed report states that around 1902, Edith returned to Idaho to visit her mother, who was living near Lenore.

When Edith reached the age of eighteen, her impetuousness led her into a short-lived marriage with William Caswell, a Boston physician. Edith kept the marriage secret to all but her closest friends. After the wedding on July 9, 1905, the couple lived together for only a few months and, later, had the union annulled. Laura Thompson died that year.

Edith May Thompson, circa 1900. *From* True Detective, *April 1930.*

Single again, Edith would suffer another terrible loss. Charles Thompson Jr., Edith's foster brother, had for some time secretly nurtured romantic desires for her. When she rejected his affections, he killed himself in 1906. She consoled herself with an engagement to Harry Adams, but then Gilbert Woodill, a California native and prosperous Los Angeles automobile dealer, came a-calling after meeting her at the Hotel Navarre. They married after a five-day romance. It was 1908. "Papa Gage" gave the couple $5,000 ($130,000) as a wedding gift and began construction of a California mansion where Edith and Gilbert could live with him.

In May 1909, Gilbert's business interests necessitated a trip to New York. Wanting to return to visit her family at their Maryland home, Edith accompanied him to the East Coast. After concluding his responsibilities in New York, the couple caught a train for McDaniel, on the east shore, across the Chesapeake from Annapolis, for what they hoped would be a restful stay with the family. Circumstances began to converge that would destroy those hopes.

Before Gilbert found himself forced to return to Los Angeles, he struck up a conversation with a middle-aged man who walked with a decided limp and had purchased an adjacent farm a few months before the Woodills arrived. Appearing highly educated and well traveled, he was already very friendly with the Thompson family. He gave his name as Emmett E. Roberts and volunteered that he was the editor of the Denver magazine *Facts* and wanted to find a quiet place to escape all the publicity that came with publishing. The Thompsons and Woodills did not know that Roberts was not the man he portrayed himself to be.

New York metropolitan police detectives were casting a net far and wide for Robert "Lame Bob" Emmett Eastman, a broker on the Consolidated Stock Exchange. When the firm of Eastman and Company failed, investigators learned that he had absconded with $200,000 ($5.2 million) of a client's money, and a grand jury indicted him for grand larceny. Eastman left his wife, Vinnie, and their newborn child in New York City and dropped out of sight in December 1908. Emmett E. Roberts was Robert Emmett Eastman. Edith did not know how dangerous this man was.

After Gilbert left for Los Angeles, Edith and Eastman began spending a lot of time together, talking of his books and her music. He was in his forties; she was twenty-two. As with so many people before him, Eastman seems to have fallen in love with Edith, who sensed their continued association might raise eyebrows in the community. She approached her father:

> *Daddy, you are sure there is no harm to my going out in Mr. Roberts' boat with him? You know how I should dislike, even innocently, to cause any comment.*

Charles assured her, "None at all, my pet." So the seemingly harmless boat trips and walks continued. Three weeks into the friendship, Edith told her stepsister Annie that she was going for some dental work in Easton, a city fourteen miles inland from the bay. Edith took a train to Royal Oak, where Eastman was seen picking her up in his horse and buggy for the last seven miles of her journey.

In later testimony, people related that Edith was wearing a tailor-made "ashes of rose" linen suit. Her pumps were bronze and had wide bronze ribbon bows. A silk ribbon belt encircled her waist, clasped with a metal buckle that was a gift from an admirer in Paris. After concluding her business in Easton, the two returned to Royal Oak, where they chartered a motor launch for the final part of the journey. Eastman ran the motorboat aground on a sand bar and could not free it, forcing them to use a rowboat borrowed from a farmer. It was Saturday night, June 19, 1909, and the last time Edith was seen alive.

Her friends and family were not concerned when she failed to return that evening, but when Monday came and Edith still was missing, Charles Thompson contacted Eastman. "I suppose you left Edith in Easton."

Edith Thompson Woodill, circa 1907. *From* True Detective, *April 1930.*

"Oh, no," was the reply. "Edith went on up to Baltimore. I thought she had told you." Colonel Thompson would later say that he had a bad feeling about the situation. On Tuesday, he put out the word to neighbors, and various stories began to merge into a bitter scenario. William Sutton, a neighbor, came forward to relate that he had visited Eastman's bungalow on Sunday, at about six o'clock, to invite him to church services that evening. As he approached the house, he could hear a man and woman in a heated argument. The woman was very angry and telling the man what she thought of him. "It was no place for churchgoers," Sutton would comment. The next morning, George Powell, another neighbor to the Eastman house, happened upon Eastman busily at work over a bonfire behind the bungalow, adding fuel and poking a stick carefully around in the embers. Later that day, Eastman went to Baltimore.

Upon his return, Eastman went out of his way to speak with Powell, explaining that he was burning straw that was used to cushion a new set of dishes for his home. He then began telling Powell an account of how friends at his home on Saturday had gotten into a violent argument. Powell was unconvinced, and he was proven correct. On Wednesday, a letter arrived from Edith, posted in Baltimore. Addressed to Annie, Edith explained that she had gone to Baltimore to see a show and wait for more dental work. "I told you so," was Eastman's only comment.

That evening, a few friends began to analyze the situation. Sutton suddenly remembered something Eatman had said to him—he had wondered how long it would take for crabs to consume a human body. They would not have to wait long to learn the truth.

Edgar and Hamilton Grace were crabbing in the shallows of the Back River on June 24 when they saw the outline of a human hand appearing above the water. Attached to the hand was the body of a young woman clad only in a silk shirt. The body had been ravaged by crabs. The skull was crushed in and the face badly disfigured. Around the woman's waist, someone had tied an iron teakettle containing a half-dozen bricks. Despite this attempt to weigh down the corpse, it had drifted with the tide into shallow water.

The last reported portrait of Edith Woodill. *From the* Los Angeles Herald, *June 26, 1909.*

At first, investigators thought the body was that of a woman who had been missing for several days. Identification would take the expertise of Thomas Smithers, the dentist Edith had visited days earlier. His diagnosis removed all doubt: these were the remains of Edith May Thompson Woodill. Eastman reacted with surprise when the news of the awful discovery was made public and even offered to travel to Baltimore to make sure the press got the story. He was unaware that the local police were closing in.

Police descended on the Eastman home, a half-completed bungalow where they found ample evidence of Eastman's guilt in the murder. Three pieces of tongue-and-groove flooring were stained with blood and held strands of Edith's hair. In the bedroom, investigators found a bloodstained sheet and a blood-soaked mattress. The floor under the bed was covered in blood. The murderer had tried to replace the flooring with wood, but the stains were more than he could hide. A blood-spattered wheelbarrow sat next to the house, replete with a bloody handprint. A scrap of paper held a vital clue: "You were seen in Baltimore Tuesday. I think the police kn—." That was all that could be read.

The Eastman house, where Edith died. *From* True Detective, *April 1930.*

Witnesses identified him as being with Edith on Saturday night. Before the authorities could question him, he fled in a boat into the bay, and the manhunt began. A posse eventually cornered Eastman, who committed suicide before they could take him into custody.

What was the motive for this brutal murder, which likely occurred in the late hours of June 20, after William Sutton had chanced upon the angry voices at the Eastman home? Some speculated that Eastman had tried to convince Edith to visit him in his home late at night or to run away with him to the anonymity of some foreign land. A colored man overheard her saying, "No, I tell you I can't go" when in company with her killer. Did Edith threaten to expose him as revenge for his indiscretions with her? Rejected romantic advances in the bungalow could have led to his whereabouts becoming known to New York police, as the scrap of paper seemed to convey. The letter from Edith to Annie had been a ruse. Eastman had even pawned her jewelry while he was in Baltimore.

No church would accept his body for its graveyard, so he was buried on his property. Edith was laid to rest next to her stepbrother, who had killed himself for love of her. Edith's mother heard the news from a reporter who found her in Ahsahka, Idaho, a small village about fifty miles by road east of Lewiston along the Clearwater River. After she composed herself, Zettella told the reporter the early story of the child who had left Idaho, become the beloved of a president and ended up food for the crabs in Chesapeake Bay.

6

A Ceremony Drowned in Passionate Intensity

Things fall apart; the centre cannot hold; Mere anarchy is loosed upon the world.
—*William Butler Yeats*

Women who initiate divorce proceedings or call it quits to a romantic relationship place themselves in danger. The National Coalition Against Domestic Violence reports that about 75 percent of the visits to emergency rooms by battered women occur after their separation from an abusive partner. Women who leave their batterers are at 75 percent greater risk of severe injury or death than those who stay. So it was for a young Lewiston mother in February 1957. No story of star-crossed lovers, this is a tale of entitlement, abuse, drunken rage and two murders.

Garnita Corrine Hazeltine was born on July 11, 1933. Her parents divorced when she was a toddler, and her mother, Dorothy, married Harold "Coach" Campbell, a successful Lewiston businessman who owned several restaurants, including the Stables and Canter's. Campbell raised Garnita as his own child. Although he never legally adopted her, Garnita took his last name as hers. After attending Garfield and Orchards Elementary Schools (*Lost Lewiston* 32, 142), Garnita blossomed to be a busy junior high school and high school student, taking part in the a cappella group, L Cube (the longtime girls service organization), the all-district chorus and the all-school play, among other activities. At five feet, ten inches, she stood out in any crowd and probably did so on May 28, when she walked through the line during the graduation ceremonies for the 140-member class of 1951.

Garnita Hazeltine Campbell, 1951. *Courtesy of Carol Servatius.*

Her best friend, Virginia Thompson Leonard, remembers how Garnita loved to attend dances in the small towns around Lewiston. The senior prophecy that appears in her yearbook says it well, "Garnita Campbell is in Clarkston. By golly, she's heading for Moscow. Oh, well, in a few years we'll catch up with her." She moved to Seattle in 1953 after attending classes at Eastern Washington College of Education (now Eastern Washington University) and began working for the Yellow Cab Company, reuniting with high school classmate Yvonne Capitan and meeting Seward Prosser. Garnita had always wanted to meet a nice guy and get married. She chose poorly.

Prosser was born in Seward, Alaska, in September 1925. He had dropped out of high school after two years and went to work as a "barn boss," probably a position where he was in charge of equipment for a company. Entering the U.S. Army in April 1944, Seward served as private for the duration of the war and for six months thereafter. In December 1947, he married for the first time at Kodiak, Alaska. A son, Michael, was born in April 1949. In a later deposition to Lewiston police, his first wife told a troubling tale:

> *He made my life unbearable. He was a heavy drinker and spent what little money he would earn on liquor and women. At the time of our marriage I was employed and continued to work until six months prior to my son's birth. Two months after Michael was born, it was necessary for me to return to work in order to provide food and shelter for my baby. All during this time, Seward kept drinking and carousing with other women, neglecting his family and apparently unconcerned there were no funds to exist on…There were at least three occasions when he became very abusive, striking me on the last one.*

Moving to Tacoma, Washington, to live with her aunt, Mrs. Prosser began working and making a new life away from Seward. Three months later, he showed up, pleading for another chance, saying that he had "straightened out." Against her better judgment, she agreed to a reconciliation, but he soon returned to his wine and women habits. When he was served with divorce papers, Seward began to harass her and her employer and threatened Michael's life. "You'll never take the baby from me. I'll see him dead first." A judge finalized the decree in February 1952. During the proceedings, Seward's mother agreed to care for Michael, but after the divorce, she claimed that the boy's mother was unfit. The court disagreed and gave Michael back to his mother.

Seward came a-courting with a lot of baggage. He was a Seattle bus driver who drove the route Garnita took to her job at the Yellow Cab Company. They began to date. Seward's first wife learned of his romantic involvement with Garnita, contacted her and warned her against becoming too involved with him. Seward, no doubt, would have claimed that he had "straightened out." Yvonne disliked him almost from the beginning and asked Garnita not to bring him to the apartment. Love is blind, they say. Heedless of the portents and against the advice of others, Garnita married Seward on March 6, 1954.

It is said that the best predictor of future behavior is past behavior. Seward could not keep a job, so Garnita was forced to be the breadwinner. If there was ever a poster child for the controlling, abusive husband, Seward fit the bill, even insisting that Garnita send child support payments to his first wife, who confirmed their receipt with Garnita's signature on the checks. The marriage was doomed from the beginning. Their situation became irreconcilable, and she returned to Lewiston with her infant daughter, Debra, in 1955 to live with her mother at 716 Tenth Street, three blocks from her old high school. Garnita found work as a comptometer (an operator of a key-driven calculator) for the Camas Prairie Railroad. Seward followed several months later and started working part time for the Great Western Wholesale Company in north Lewiston, renting a basement apartment at 620 Fifth Street. Albert "Blackie" Furest, whom Dorothy had recently married, remembered that the couple sparred for several months.

Idaho's divorce laws have always been exceptionally lenient, requiring only six weeks of residency to become eligible. As a result, the state has been the venue for several high-profile divorces. Katherine Rush, a wealthy Chicago socialite, moved to Lewiston in 1910 to establish Idaho residency, living with the John Bender family. A local attorney, Bender was, at the time, also president of the chamber of commerce. In November, Rush filed for divorce from her husband, famed Chicago attorney George Rush. In May 1963, presidential candidate Nelson Rockefeller married Margaretta "Happy" Murphy, who had taken a six-week vacation in Sun Valley to obtain a divorce. His public opinion ratings took a nosedive, and Barry Goldwater won the Republican nomination.

By the beginning of 1957, Garnita was ready to cut Seward loose for good. Working with longtime Lewiston attorney Paul Keeton, she filed for divorce on February 4, citing extreme cruelty and seeking custody of Debra, the distribution of their community property and $50 ($425) a month for support. A temporary restraining order was issued against Seward. Garnita got her "quickie divorce." The district court granted the decree on Wednesday, February 27. The joy at her new freedom would be short-lived.

Seward arrived at work the next morning but by lunchtime asked his boss for the rest of the day off. He did not go home. About noon, he entered Bojack's Club, a popular bar at 311 Main Street. After two or three beers, he ordered lunch to be delivered by cab from the Majestic Café, a longtime Chinese restaurant once found in the 800 block of Main Street. After a meal and a total of six beers, Seward left around 2:30 p.m. and headed east on Main Street. Johnny Miller, on duty at the Star Second Hand Store at Delsol and Main, greeted Seward as he entered a little after 3:00 p.m. Seward wanted to buy a "cheap gun."

When Miller showed him a .32 Colt automatic, Seward said that he wanted to purchase it for his wife, as he was working nights and going out of town on a job. When Miller asked Seward for his name for the bill, he gave "Lund," with an address of 716 Fourteenth Street, which was actually the address of one of Garnita's friends with whom she went bowling on Thursday evenings. It was Thursday. Seward told Miller that his wife got off work at 4:30 p.m. He would show her the pistol. If she did not like it, he would bring it back and trade it for another. The total bill, including a box of ammunition, came to $29.40 ($250).

By 6:30 p.m., Seward was back at Bojack's, where he encountered Ted Piche, the club's bartender, who had attended Seward's marriage to Garnita. He ordered up a couple of drinks, had a barmaid go to the nearby liquor store for a pint of whiskey and purchased a large bottle of 7 Up. By 7:00 p.m., he had left, presumably to attend a party somewhere in town. Getting into his 1955 Nash Metropolitan, Seward drove around town, ending up at the Furest home on Tenth Street shortly before 8:00 p.m. He parked in front of the house and sat for a few minutes before approaching the home.

A crime scene photo at the Furest home. *Courtesy of the Lewiston Police Department.*

Seward knocked at the door. Garnita answered and invited him in, offering him a cup of coffee. Dorothy Furest, Garnita's mother, who was sitting across the room, began to assail him with epithets I will not repeat here. Looking at his now ex-wife, Seward asked her why she allowed her mother to say such things. "That is what you are," Garnita replied as she stood and told him that he had better leave. As he rose, he pulled the pistol from his top coat pocket and shot her twice. Garnita said nothing, turned and walked onto the porch, collapsing into the shrubbery next to the steps.

Seward turned to Dorothy, who was approaching him with scissors in her hand. Two more shots rang out, and she fell near the sewing machine. Placing the Colt back into his pocket, he made his way past Dorothy's body to a bedroom where his infant daughter, Debra, was still asleep. The gunshots had not disturbed her slumber. He kissed her and left the house, stopping at Garnita's body. His plan of killing himself in front of her had gone awry. He drove back to his apartment on Fifth Street and knocked on the door of his neighbor, Maria Michalick, who takes up this narrative:

> *He came to my apartment about 8:00 p.m. and said they probably would not see him again. He said he was going to California. He had a pint of*

whiskey with him and a large bottle of 7 Up. The bottle was not opened. Prosser was crying at this time. He continued to cry all the time he was in my apartment. He asked for something he could pour some of the whiskey into. I told him I did not have anything. He opened the bottle and poured the contents down the sink and filled the bottle with 7 Up. He was only here a few minutes when he got ready to go. He asked me if I went to church. I said, "Sometimes, but not as much as Gloria, my daughter, does." He then asked if Gloria would pray for him. Then he went out. He sat in his car for a few minutes, slumped over the wheel. I believe he was crying at that time. Then he left.

Seward returned to Bojack's, arriving about 8:30 p.m. The bartender noticed that with the change Seward pulled from his pocket to buy a drink, there were two .32 cartridges. "He seemed," Piche would later recount, "more at ease at that time than he had for a long time." Seward called for a taxi, shook hands with Piche and said, "It has been nice knowing you and having you as a friend. See you in Hell."

Driver Charles Bedard answered the dispatcher's call for a passenger at the bar. When he arrived, he found Seward "pretty well loaded" and drinking heavily. At first, Seward told Bedard that he just wanted to ride around but soon directed him to Tenth Street. As they neared the house, Seward told him to "turn the lights off and drive slow." After passing the home, Prosser asked Bedard to drive by again and stop. Seward got out and walked up to the front steps, where he bent forward and appeared to be feeling around for something where Garnita lay.

As Seward entered the house, Bedard exited his cab and walked toward the home. It was then that he saw a woman's leg sticking over the front steps. A car pulled up with two women inside. They were Norma McCrery and Geneva Peterson, who had arrived to pick up Garnita to go bowling. When Bedard told them that a woman was lying in the shrubs, they became frightened and quickly drove away. When they reached the end of the block, the women heard a shot. Their telephone call would be the first alert the police would receive.

Seward came out of the house soon after McCrery and Peterson drove off. Bedard asked Seward what was wrong with the woman by the porch. "Oh, she's just drunk," he replied. As the two men neared the taxi, "Blackie" Furest appeared on the front porch. He said, "Which one of you SOBs hit her?" Furest charged at Seward, who pulled the Colt from his pocket and fired again, the shot that McCrery and Peterson heard. Wounded in the

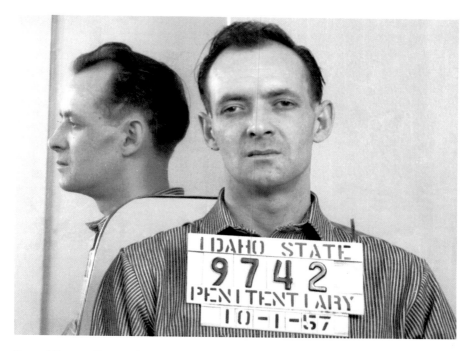

Seward Prosser. *Courtesy of the Idaho State Historical Society, AR42 #9742.*

groin, Blackie retreated to the south side of the house, and Seward jumped into the cab.

"I just killed my wife and mother-in-law. If you don't keep your mouth shut, I'll blow your brain out," he told Bedard.

They drove back to Bojack's, and Seward quickly went into the men's room to go through a purse he had taken from the house, presumably looking for money to pay for his trip to California. He had thrown the purse from the cab while en route. A "good Samaritan" returned it to Seward before he entered the bar. The police were soon in the establishment, taking Seward into custody without incident.

At the house, officers found Debra screaming in her crib amidst the chaos that met them: two bodies and a man bleeding badly. A neighbor quieted Debra and took her home. Blackie would spend days in the hospital, but he survived.

Seward signed a full confession the morning after his arrest and would sit in the county jail for several months, finally pleading guilty to second-degree murder in September in a plea bargain. Judge John Cramer handed down two concurrent twenty-year sentences.

Prosecuting attorney Wynne Blake agreed to the adjusted charge because Prosser was highly intoxicated, and he doubted that a jury would convict him of first-degree murder. Paroled in 1963, Prosser moved to Oregon, where he remarried in 1970 and died on October 23, 1978. His burial in the Willamette National Cemetery angered those who knew and loved the vivacious Lewiston girl who had married so badly.

And what of the baby? Debra became the focus of a nasty child custody battle once again orchestrated by Seward's mother. Garnita's relatives and Seward's first wife rallied to ensure that the little girl would have a loving home, which proved to be with her great-aunt Betty in California. It was what Garnita had always wanted.

On April 5, 1940, Jack Oppedahl chose a permanent solution to what must have been a temporary problem. A Norwegian immigrant and local logger, Jack's choice was the inbound Northern Pacific passenger train making its run from Lewiston to Spokane. Eli Joliff was passing along the right of way and spoke to Oppedahl but got no reply.

As Joliff and a friend were standing next to the railroad icehouse, they looked around as the train passed. It was then that Oppedahl got up and walked close to the tracks. As the train neared him, Oppedahl quickened his pace. When the engine was about thirty to forty feet away, he threw himself across the track. The train was traveling only fifteen miles per hour, as it was coming into the Lewiston depot. Engineer E.J. Holmes saw Oppedahl approaching and his fatal leap but could not stop the train, even with the emergency brake engaged.

Of course, a crowd gathered at the scene until the body was removed to Brower-Wann Funeral Home (*Hidden History* 102).

7

DESPOILERS, DESPERADOS AND THE OTHER USUAL SUSPECTS

The more laws and order are made prominent, the more thieves and robbers there will be.
—Lao Tzu

Highwaymen, ruffians and other criminal riffraff populated Lewiston from the beginning. Their aims were always the same; only the tools and technology changed over the decades. The region centering on Lewiston was a very dangerous place to live. Four murders were committed in two weeks in Lewiston in the fall of 1861. Home invasions were not uncommon. Ned Meany was shot dead in a quarrel just outside of town in November. In December, two masked intruders entered a house and got away with $500 ($13,000), killing one of the inhabitants.

Early criminals could be less than gracious even in captivity. Take, for example, the case of Christopher Lower, one of the men convicted in the murders of Lloyd Magruder and his companions in October 1863. Someone got the bright idea of having photographs taken of the prisoners. Officials spoke with Lower, James Romain and David Renton. The trio would have nothing to do with the idea. After several more attempts, Lower said that he would agree to sit for a portrait. Word was sent to Walla Walla, and a photographer caught a steamer, arriving soon after with his equipment, which he set up in a tent near the Luna House Hotel.

Third and C Streets, 1862, showing a tent (left center) thought to be a photography studio from 1864 to 1866. *Courtesy of Special Collections and Archives, University of Idaho Library, 5-007-4a.*

Lower was escorted from the jail on First Street and sat down, posing quite willingly. When everything was ready, the photographer stepped into his dark room to install his wet plate. Unexpectedly, Lower jumped up, rushed over to the camera and smashed it to the ground. "Why did you do that, Lower?" exclaimed the sheriff. With a devilish grin, he replied, "I though it was loaded." There would be no further attempts to record the images of the first men to be hanged by an Idaho court. Fortunately, we do have some photographs of other criminals who walked Lewiston's streets or victimized people who called it home.

Although the reader might conclude that Lewiston was the sinkhole of the territory, statistics compiled by historians at the old state penitentiary tell another story. Well, at least another version. Analyzing data for inmates from 1866 to 1947 produced the finding that Nez Perce County is actually fifth on the list, behind Ada, Bannock, Canyon and Twin Falls. Unfortunately, Nez Perce County's per capita ranking is another matter.

The following is an abbreviated compendium of cases that were the "news fit to print" in the pages of city and regional newspapers about the wild and woolly town.

1870

In 1869, James Wood was working for Thomas Duffy, who ran pack trains between Lewiston and the mining camps to the east and south. The two argued over a wage settlement that Duffy thought was equitable. Feeling cheated, Wood attacked him in a fit of rage, stabbing his boss repeatedly in the back with a large knife. Duffy died within minutes. After a trial in the old Nez Perce County Courthouse that once sat on First Street, where the Lewis-Clark Hotel is now located, Wood was sentenced to death by hanging at the state penitentiary, which was the Boise County jail at that time.

He had spent months in the jail adjoining the courthouse when, on January 1, his sentence was commuted to life in prison by territorial governor David Ballard after pressure was evidently applied by political connections Wood had in the East. He was scheduled to be transported to Boise to serve out his new sentence, but residents of Lewiston had long before decided that he was not leaving the town alive.

About 4:00 p.m. on January 13, a group of armed men disguised as members of the Nez Perce tribe approached the jail. While several "Indians" held the jailor captive, the others took Wood to an abandoned building near the confluence of the Snake and Clearwater Rivers and hanged him. The mob felt that the original verdict fit the crime, and no easily influenced Boise politician was going to change it.

Old territorial prison and Nez Perce County jail, 1861–82. The drawing is based on the memories of Lewiston pioneers. *From* River of No Return *(1947)*.

This story did not end in 1870. Wood left his new wife, Sarah, whom he had married in August 1869. On September 12, 1902, Mary Wilson was adjudged to be insane by the court in Lewiston and was prepared for transfer to the new asylum in Blackfoot. She had been assessed two years before as being mentally unfit but seemed to have been cured. Addiction to morphine and cocaine no doubt contributed to her current condition. Wilson was one of the five Duffy children left without a father when he was murdered.

1871

A man named Walters lay in the Lewiston jail, waiting for his execution on June 9. Much to the chagrin of Lewiston residents, town marshal Daniel McElwee failed to perform his duty to carry out the sentence. The district attorney had convinced McElwee that the verdict had been arrived at illegally. Therefore, the sentence also was illegal, and he should disregard the order to execute Walters.

Another local group of "Indians" gathered and forced the jail open, taking Walters to a necktie party. Ironically, the gallows that had been erected for the original execution had been dismantled by Walters' friends. The vigilantes found another suitable and convenient crossbeam. Undeterred, McElwee continued to serve until 1873.

1882

John Akins arrived in Lewiston in February 1879. His family briefly rented the pioneer cabin that has been preserved in front of Lewiston City Hall. John would become one of the most famous steamboat captains on the Snake River in the early years of the twentieth century. But in 1882, he was still a boy and wanted to go to work. His father recommended that John contact Alfred Damas, whose store once sat on the corner of First and Main Streets. John also found employment in the bakery of Seraphin Wildenthaler (*Lost Lewiston* 56), as well as at a local saloon, often recounting a time when the local whiskey supply dried up.

One of Akins' favorite stories from his youth concerned the capture of three horse thieves, who were then regarded as public enemies and dealt quickly with frontier justice (*Hidden History* 130). One afternoon, John happened upon Wildenthaler cutting down two tall posts on his property that had been appropriated for summary executions. When John asked Serpahin what he was doing, the old man replied, "I don't want any more men hanged in my front yard."

1893

Lewiston's vigilante legacy did not end with the coming of its churches and schools. Albert Roberts had been working as a laborer with John Sutherland and his brother near Leland, Idaho, a small farming community thirty miles east of town. The Sutherlands fired Roberts and withheld $5 ($120) in pay over a dispute they were having about $20 ($600) that Roberts had reportedly stolen. In December 1892, Roberts confronted Sutherland in town, and a fistfight broke out. He got Sutherland in a headlock, pulled his revolver and killed him with three shots to the abdomen.

Roberts was immediately arrested, brought to Lewiston and booked into the county jail. On January 2, a masked group of probably a dozen men arrived at the jail and forced its way in, overpowering Deputy Sheriff W.W. Wright and Timothy Ryan. The vigilantes went to Roberts' cell and gagged him. At least two of the group guarded Wright and Ryan in the courthouse while their companions whisked Roberts out of the small jailhouse. After giving the abductors time to get a safe distance away, the guards threw Wright and Ryan into a room and lit out.

The deputy and his companion ran to their offices at the courthouse, got their revolvers and fired several shots in succession to raise the alarm that things had run amok at Main and Lapwai (now Thirteenth) Streets. The mob made its escape with Roberts, whose warm but lifeless body, bound hands and feet, was found at Wesley Mulkey's mill (near the site of the old train station). The mob had melted back into the community.

The search for the perpetrators was, at best, rudimentary, half-hearted and strictly for the town's public image—the Mulkey mill was just across the street from the courthouse. No one in the mob was ever identified, but many of the names likely would have been very familiar to Lewiston residents. Frontier justice had been meted out. In May 1995, Lewiston would be stunned by yet another case of taking the law into one's own hands, but that is a story too new, too raw and too complex to discuss in the confines of this book.

1897

The body of John Levi, a noted Nez Perce Indian, was found lying in a muddy road on March 5. He had been in Lewiston until late into the evening and was returning to Lapwai when he seems to have been waylaid and shot by some unknown assailant. John was proprietor of "Levi's Hell," an Indian gambling resort, and was accused of buncoing (running a confidence game) and robbing the tribal members who visited his house.

Levi had recently been a principal in an attempted holdup in which John Jones, an Indian enemy, was badly wounded with a knife wielded by Levi. Rumor had it that some threats had been made after the brouhaha. These facts led to the belief that the Nez Perce committed the murder, and Jones was suspected by law enforcement but never charged. At the time of his death, Levi was under a bond of $1,000 ($28,000) to appear on a charge of highway robbery.

1902

In November, Lewiston police officials were at their wits' end searching for clues that might lead to the apprehension of a felon operating on Normal Hill. A close watch had been put in place in the residential area since an attack on county commissioner Charles Leeper (*Hidden History* 81). No suspicious characters had been noticed, but a number of young women, probably college students, had been frightened by two men. On several occasions, young women were accosted by someone who stepped from the darkness. At that point, only one had been physically assaulted.

The police had some strange explanations. Robbery did not seem to be the object of the confrontations. For some unexplained reason, it was generally thought that this was the work of some jealous husband who was spying on his wife. Does that make sense to you? Were these cases of pranks perpetrated by the boys of Reid Hall (*Hidden History* 25)?

1908

East Lewiston was once popularly known as "Little Italy" because of the many Italian families that managed vegetable farms. The word "paisano," meaning compatriot, is a common one among Italians and Italian Americans. Someone should have reminded three robbers of that on January 7. Breaking down a door to gain entrance to a building, the men pummeled Pietro Tannerrasso, a local laborer. The assailants left him senseless and robbed him of $180 ($4,700), which he had saved for a trip back to his homeland.

Pietro had been sleeping peacefully and was the lone occupant of the old building when the men broke in shortly after 1:00 a.m. and left him on the floor. After regaining consciousness, he crawled out and notified his neighbors, who called police and took him to St. Joseph's Hospital for treatment. Sheriff Harry Lydon surmised that the robbers were fellow Italians who had learned of Pietro's wealth.

1928

Some criminal acts are stealthy; others are just brazen. On November 21, C.E. Blyton, a former Lewiston businessman visiting from Grand Orchards, Washington, was brutally attacked by two masked gunmen on a downtown street during the dinner hour. Blyton ended up at the White Hospital on Main Street in critical condition.

The robbers got away with $690 ($9,500) in currency, a $75 ($1,100) check and a warranty deed. Blyton could give the police little to go on. He was passing an old barn across the street from the post office at F and Twelfth Streets (now city hall) when one of the men stepped out and dragged him inside the building. After robbing him, the men beat him into unconsciousness with a blunt instrument. When he came to his senses, Blyton called out for assistance but could not tell officers which way the men went.

A suspect was arrested the next day using the few details Blyton could recall, but the man was later released.

1931

Business at Lewiston's Riverside Garage turned out to be anything but normal in October. On Wednesday, the fourteenth, two men held up the garage for $40 ($550), telling the attendant, Charles Greenhaigh, that they would kill him if he told anyone about the theft. Just to make sure, they took

Greenhaigh with them, letting him out at the top of the Lewiston Spiral Highway. The criminals must have thought that any heist that easy deserved repeating. As a result, they returned with a friend about midnight on October 20. Things were not so quiet the second time around.

After robbing Greenhaigh, the pair kidnapped him again for use as a hostage and stole a new Cadilllac. While one man watched Greenhaigh, the other two moved across the street to the Bennett Garage, once found where the city library is now located. The robbers forced attendant Virgil Wampler to the floor and prepared to leave with $60 ($830), firing a warning shot at Wampler from a Buick they appropriated. What the pair did not know

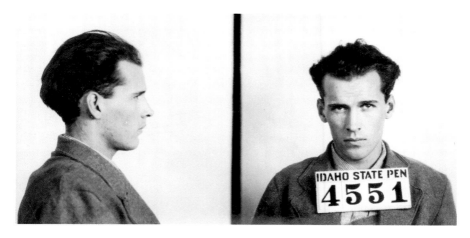

Thomas Blair. *Courtesy of the Idaho State Historical Society, AR42 #4551.*

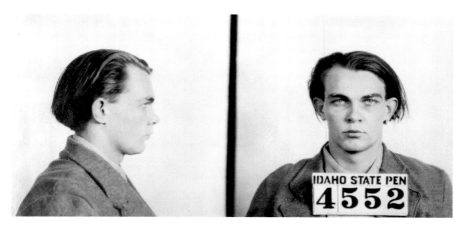

Lloyd Burns. *Courtesy of the Idaho State Historical Society, AR42 #4552.*

was that Virgil was, as they say, "packing heat." He opened up with two automatic pistols as the criminals sped away with Greenhaigh.

The police came close to stopping the thieves, but once on the open road of the Palouse prairie, the Cadillac easily outran the Plymouths the police drove. Greenhaigh later told officials:

I didn't do anything but what they told me. I wanted to get along with them. All of them had been drinking some, but the man at the wheel was a fine driver and his high speed didn't worry me. There was no dash light, but at times they made me look away and lighted matches to check the speedometer reading. They said sometimes they were doing 80 miles an hour.

Greenhaigh was finally released near Cheney, Washington, at 7:45 a.m. the next day. He quickly located a telephone and alerted Spokane police, who threw up roadblocks. Thomas Blair and Lloyd Burns were later picked up and confessed to the Lewiston capers. Blair told Lewiston officers that they liked Charles. He said, "Gee, we hated to let him [Charles] out so far from Spokane, but we were afraid to keep him with us." They gave Greenhaigh money enough to get back to Lewiston. Charles had slipped a $20 bill he had on him into his shoe to avoid discovery.

1932

Henry Gusman was a man with a track record of controversy and scandal. Born in Russia, he came to the United States in 1913 and drove a city bus for a time in Spokane, Washington. He came to Lewiston in April 1920 and opened an auto parts store. He was denied citizenship in 1922 and 1923, first for not having sufficient residency and then because he claimed an exception from the First World War because he was an alien resident.

In 1923, he was the proprietor of Lewiston Auto Parts, located in the building at Third and Main Streets that was once the Moxley Drug Store (*Hidden History* 129). Prior events caught up with him on September 1. Henry was a young man who had sown some wild oats; it turned out to be a bitter harvest.

Henry and Gertrude Jess met in Lewiston. She was working as a housemaid. Their relationship became intimate and led to Gertrude's pregnancy. To avoid scandal, Gertrude moved to Spokane and delivered a baby girl. Henry agreed to a monetary settlement to care for Gertrude and the child. The agreement seemed to be working. Henry married Anna Lillian Colen on July 3, 1922, in Spokane. Anna was also a Russian immigrant.

On Friday, August 31, 1923, Gertrude showed up at Henry's store with their eighteen-month-old child, complaining about the agreement. Their meeting did not go well. She left after making threats against Gusman and their child. She went to a nearby pharmacy and purchased carbolic acid. When the clerk asked her why she wanted carbolic, she replied that she needed a disinfectant.

On Saturday morning, Gertrude arrived at the auto parts store again and asked Henry for his forgiveness for what she had said the previous day. Henry reminded her that things had been satisfactorily settled between them two years earlier and that, as far as he was concerned, the matter was closed, per a legal agreement. That was not what Gertrude wanted to hear.

She did not speak for a moment and then pulled out the two-ounce vial of acid and drank it, falling to the floor with the baby in her arms. Some of the caustic liquid spilled from her mouth onto the child's face and under its arms. Henry immediately summoned fire chief Vern Westfall from the

Vern Westfall (in passenger seat wearing white helmet), 1910. *Courtesy of the Lewiston Fire Department.*

station a block away. Westfall rushed Gertrude and her baby to the White Hospital (*Lost Lewiston* 42) "in a record run." Dr. Edgar White treated the wounds, keeping Gertrude at the hospital for two weeks. Her father, a well-known farmer in the Keuterville area on the Camas Prairie, came to take mother and child home.

Henry finally achieved his goal of citizenship on November 20, 1924. Retaining ownership of the auto parts store, Henry, Anna and their young son, James, moved in 1929 to Boise, where he founded the Idaho Equipment Company. You would think that Henry had had enough excitement in his life, but no, he was about to walk too close to the edge again and would be returning to Lewiston.

The Idaho Equipment Company began to prosper with state contracts, especially those with the state highway department. In March 1932, a grand jury handed down a seven-point indictment charging Gusman with fraud. The number of counts finally reached forty-two. In November 1931, Idaho governor Ben Ross had fired Alvin Harbour, the commissioner of public works. An internal investigation discovered that Idaho had been overcharged thousands of dollars a month for equipment purchases. Guess who was the supplier to whom the inflated prices were paid. It was estimated that as much as $300,000 ($4.2 million) was pocketed in the scheme.

When the matter came to trial in the spring of 1932, the state prosecutor had little trouble connecting all of the dots. Gusman's co-conspirator had kept a "little black book" cataloging all of their dealings. Convicted on April 29, Henry received a sentence of two and a half to five years in the state

Henry Gusman. *Courtesy of the Idaho State Historical Society, AR42 #4621.*

penitentiary, as well as a $5,000 ($90,000) fine. On July 5, 1933, the state board of pardons denied him clemency.

In November, Gusman notified the state parole board that he intended to again ask for a pardon. Henry felt that since he had been convicted on losses of less than $300 ($3,500), he had served enough time. What he failed to admit was that forty more indictments were outstanding at the time of his conviction. When he paid his fine, the other charges were dropped. Again, Henry did not get a hearing ear from the board.

In December 1933, Henry's name was again in the newspapers when George Rudd, the warden of the state penitentiary, was accused by Franklin Girard, the Idaho secretary of state and a member of the prison board, of taking prisoners, including Gusman, from the facility on trips about the state. Nez Perce County officials lobbied against his early release, which occurred in June 1934.

Henry, Anna and James moved to San Francisco, California, after his release from prison. In the 1940 federal census, he is listed as the president of a new building equipment company. He died on September 25, 1965, at the age of sixty-seven.

1934

The Firestone store on the corner of D and Ninth Streets was a busy place for many years. No day was busier than October 2. Two bandits walked in at noon, drew their guns and ordered bookkeeper Howard Keinle to turn over the cash or risk being "plugged." Four employers were in the building at the time but because of their duties knew nothing of what was transpiring in the office. Wesley Steele, a mechanic, later testified that he was under a car and did not even hear Keinle call out that they had been robbed. He was surprised to see police chief Eugene Gasser come running into the garage after the heist was pulled off.

The robbers demanded that the bookkeeper open the safe, but he told them that there was no money in it. The taller of the two culprits stepped behind the counter and began rifling through the cash register, from which he removed $180 ($3,200) in cash and $25 ($450) in checks. The felons then took off on foot east on D Street and were out of sight before police officers could even be notified. Police unsuccessfully searched the hobo "jungles" on Holbrook Island and several "rooming houses." Two hours after the robbery, two young men on a motorcycle were detained in Pomeroy, Washington, thirty miles west of the city. However, the men proved their innocence and were released. It was a clean getaway.

1934

A card game among friends went very bad on Thursday, October 25. Compton "Tobin" Morgan, a thirty-year-old itinerant black man, had joined several black companions for an evening of cards in the rear room of a Chinese store located on old Sixth Street, near the current site of the *Lewiston Tribune*, which was Lewiston's Chinatown from the 1890s to 1940s. A fight broke out, and some pretty harsh words were uttered. Jim Thomas reportedly picked up a chair and was about to strike Morgan, who reacted by wielding his knife and plunging it into Thomas' chest. Jim died the next Monday at the White Hospital.

Tobin fled Lewiston after the stabbing but was soon arrested in Yakima, Washington.

The police investigators determined that Morgan was never in any serious danger and could have easily retreated. The principles of self-defense state that one must retreat unless retreating will increase your level of danger. Morgan could not plead that to be the case. Therefore, he entered a guilty

Compton Morgan. *Courtesy of the Idaho State Historical Society, AR42 #5023.*

plea. Tobin had no criminal background and was "highly penitent" for what he had done to his friend. The court could find no evidence of premeditation and gave him ten to twenty years for second-degree murder on November 4. "You are a very clever actor," Judge Miles Johnson said, "or your penitence is genuine."

1935

For more than two weeks in June, a lone bandit terrorized motorists in and around Lewiston, sneaking up to parked cars and, at the point of a gun, relieving them of their money and valuables (*Hidden History* 138–139). Night after night, local police officers, as well as those from neighboring counties, trailed him without success.

On June 25, Lewiston police officers Andrew Verzani and Ollie Arbelbide drove to a lonely road near Uniontown, Washington, and set up what they hoped would be a successful sting. They waited for more than an hour in the dark, when the headlights of an oncoming car revealed the figure of a lone pedestrian who jumped into the weeds at the side of the road when the other car got near. The man got up and approached Verzani's car. When Verzani ordered the man to halt, he started to flee. Verzani fired a warning shot. To his surprise, he heard a bullet whiz by his head.

Ed Miles. *Courtesy of the Idaho State Historical Society, AR42 #5128.*

Arbelbide fired twice with his sawed-off shotgun. Verzani finally trained his flashlight on the fleeing criminal, later identified as Ed Miles (aka Edward Robert Cain, Edward J. Dillon Miles and Edward Cain) and fired. The bullet struck Miles in the face, tearing out his upper teeth and knocking him to the ground.

Verzani handcuffed Miles and stripped him of a loaded cartridge belt, revolver, field glasses and $16 ($220) in cash. Dr. Elmer Braddock came to the police station on Third Street to treat Miles' wounds. Through his bandages, Miles mumbled that he had been in Lewiston and, unable to find work, had resorted to robbery to buy food. Let us hope he enjoyed the food at the county jail. When he was arraigned before probate judge John Phillips, Miles demanded a preliminary hearing. Phillips agreed and set his bond at $20,000 ($275,000). Ed was a "bad boy," known to prison officials in several states, including California, where he had served time at Folsom for robbery.

Showing no remorse and vowing to get revenge on Verzani, Miles received a sentence of twenty to forty years in the state penitentiary, from which he escaped on May 8, 1937, after sawing his way out of his cell and scaling the prison wall. Warden William Gess described Miles as "one of the most desperate criminals we have had at the Idaho Prison."

Freedom was fleeting. He was captured in Phoenix, Arizona, in October.

1935

Thirty-three-year-old Florence Coleman, formerly Mrs. Kitoff, found herself in the county jail on October 1, lacking the $10,000 ($175,000) to pay her bail. A local barber, she did not have that kind of cash. What's more, authorities in Idaho and Washington debated whether to try her for assaulting her husband or to return her to prison for shooting her former brother-in-law. She had been arrested after stabbing her husband, W.B. Coleman, a disabled World War I veteran, in the abdomen and leg with a butcher knife.

When the news of the attack made the newspapers, the Washington State Parole Office informed Idaho authorities that they wanted her for violating her parole from state prison on September 16. Washington was intent on sending her back to the Walla Walla penitentiary to resume serving her sentence. Florence had calmly leaned out of a parked car and killed Paul Kitoff, her husband Mike's brother, on May 23, 1931, in front of her husband's Seattle soda parlor. Police thought that she may have been aiming for Mike, but when interviewed, she said, "I shot straight and got the man I wanted."

At first, Florence claimed Paul was preventing a reunion with her husband, but during the trial, she blamed beatings she said her husband had inflicted on her for her temporary insanity. Prosecutor Cordelia Thiel exclaimed, "[She] has no right to be at large. She should be removed from society. This jury has just as much right to take her life as she had to take Paul Kitoff's life." The jury of five women and seven men ruled for manslaughter, and Florence got a sentence of five to twenty years. Mike assisted with the state's case but did not testify. He divorced her in December 1934, while she was in prison.

A little quick math shows that she had been out of prison for only two weeks, remarried and attempted to kill her new husband. Does the term "black widow" bring an image to mind? Florence took back her maiden name (Vadnais) and died in Yakima, Washington, in March 1975.

The butcher knife method seemed to be the modus of choice. On February 4, 1906, William Yarbaugh struck his wife with a butcher knife and then attempted to commit suicide. He was bound over for trial on charges of attempted murder. He sat it out in jail, as he could not raise the $1,500 ($40,000) bail and was probably set to work sweeping streets.

1949

On July 19, retired Potlatch Forests Inc. logger George Lecovich was found dead with his hands bound in front of his chest with a cheap black and red necktie on the shore of the Clearwater River behind 1603 Main Street, the location of the Lewiston Marble and Granite Works. His body was discovered by Lester Bray, a twenty-nine-year-old transient who was living in a nearby wrecked 1928 Chevrolet sedan. Lester had gone to the river to wash his hands and face at 6:00 a.m.

Lecovich had been living in the old Frye Hotel at 1122 Main Street and was under the care of a Lewiston physician for heart disease. A large abrasion could be seen on his head, and one tooth had been knocked out. The necktie had been knotted several times. This was no suicide. The last person to see Lecovich alive was Stella Huff, his landlady at the hotel, at about 7:00 p.m. She noticed no change in his demeanor, and no one came forward to say they had seen him later.

Robbery as a motive entered the investigation when Lecovich's wallet, which he was known to carry in his pocket, was missing. The police offered a reward for its discovery. The timing of his death took on a truly CSI nature, even for 1949. The evidence pointed to Lecovich being *in* and *out* of the water. How was that possible? He had not drowned. The answer lay in the Washington Water Power dam that once spanned the Clearwater River at what is now Clearwater Paper Company (*Historic Firsts* 161). Crews at the dam had opened and closed the gates during the night, as heavy equipment was moved into place for a project.

The water level rose between 10:00 p.m. and 2:00 a.m. As George's clothes were wet, coroner Andrew Vassar ruled that the body had been in the river. George's watch was full of water and stopped at 11:18 p.m. In Vassar's opinion, Lecovich was either thrown or placed into the river, his assailant expecting that his body would be washed away. However, the current was not strong enough in the low water days of summer. The time of death was between 9:00 p.m. and 11:00 p.m.

The crime scene was a jumbled confusion of dank undergrowth and rusty automobile shells used by transients as homes. The area was littered with empty beer, wine and whiskey bottles; campfire pits; and girly magazines. Only one tree provided any shade. The path to the river's edge was cluttered by driftwood and old timbers that eluded the sawmill's pond monkeys. There were no signs that the body had been dragged. The police were at a loss about the attacker's identity but did agree that whoever it was did not intend to kill Lecovich. According to the doctor, the least bit of violence could have killed him.

Eventually, the case was labeled a "jungletown" death, so-called for the area of town near and on Holbrook Island known to locals as a hobo jungle where the homeless took refuge. The crime was never solved. Holbrook Island was submerged when the pool behind Lower Granite Dam was filled in 1975.

1949

Gunfire broke out after two customers at Chuck's Place, a tavern located at 1522 Main Street, challenged a robber on November 24. A masked man entered the bar about 11:30 p.m. and threatened Gladys Keller, the bartender. "He just pointed the gun at me," she reported to police.

Chuck's Place, circa 1960. *Courtesy of the Nez Perce County Historical Society.*

Charles Lemmons and John Hendley stepped in and were killed for their efforts.

George Jensen, a construction worker, was apprehended with an accomplice at a Lewiston hotel only a few blocks from the scene of the shooting after Lewiston police got an anonymous tip. Jensen was charged with first-degree murder and pleaded guilty. It was later discovered that he was actually George Martin and was an escapee for the Washington State Prison. He was sentenced to life at the Idaho Penitentiary on December 3 but returned to Washington. Ironically, Hendley had survived three years of combat in World War II, earning seven battle stars while serving with George Patton's tank division.

1951

A janitor coming to work on an evening not on his normal schedule probably frightened off thieves who had broken into Cecil's Club at 912 Main Street in the early morning hours of Christmas Day. At the time of the robbery, losses were estimated to be between $500 ($4,600) and $8,000 ($73,000). C.W. Milligan arrived at the club at 1:20 a.m. and found that the back door had been breached with a crow bar. Investigating officers noted that the safe's dial had been forced off but repeated hammering had failed to open it.

Three rings of slot machine keys were lying on the bar. Mulligan's arrival must have scared the robbers before they had a chance to open the machines. Slots were very common in Lewiston bars and clubs (*Hidden History* 128).

1952

A convicted bank robber was shot to death by a Lewiston police officer in an early morning gun battle at Eleventh and Main Streets on August 11.

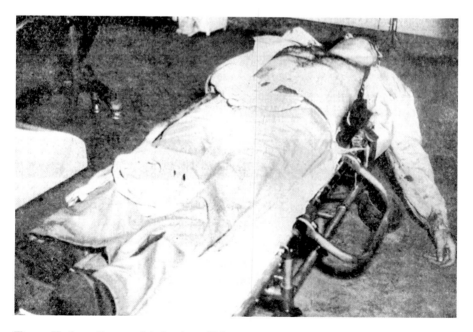

Turner Hudson. *Courtesy of the* Lewiston Tribune.

Killed was Turner Hudson, aged forty-three. Shortly before midnight, a local couple heard noises and saw two men crouching in the shadows in an attempt to hide. When three officers arrived, they dropped off patrolman Edward "Bud" Lucas to investigate on foot while the other two used their car to cruise the neighborhood and possibly flush out the suspects.

Hudson began running toward Main Street and was confronted by Lucas. Hudson pulled a .357 Magnum from his coat pocket and fired once at the officer, hitting the pavement in front of him. Lucas returned fire with his .38 service revolver, hitting Hudson in the right eye and killing him instantly as the bullet passed through his brain and out the left side of his skull. Lucas described the encounter:

> *As I started into* [the Snappy Service lot], *I saw a fellow running. We almost hit head-on, and he had his hand inside his shirt. I told him to stop. He began running sideways in a crouched position and pulled out his gun and shot. I went for mine and shot, too. That's all.*

An investigation showed that Hudson and his partner were probably preparing to burgle several sites in Lewiston, as his 1951 Mercury was filled with safecracking equipment. A coroner's inquest that week found no cause to bring charges against Officer Lucas. Hudson's accomplice escaped.

1952

You have heard of the expression "an eye for an eye." Well, on September 29, the saying took on personal meaning for a Clarkston man turned robber.

At 11:26 p.m., Robert Shoemake walked into Millie's Tavern at 212 Main Street, across the street from

Robert Shoemake. *Courtesy of the Idaho State Historical Society, AR42 #7191.*

the Hotel Lewis-Clark. Shoemake did not even bother to rifle the cash register, as had been done in 1934, when the Firestone store was robbed. He just picked up the register and headed outside to a car where an accomplice was waiting. When he got to the door, he dropped the register as he was struggling with Mrs. William Blasingame, the wife of the owner, who suffered a knife wound in the altercation. One female patron slugged him with a beer glass.

The clumsy robbers sped off at high speed and crashed into a truck carrying horses half a mile east of the tavern. Police finally ran the car into the curb at Sixteenth and Main Streets. Shoemake was transported to St. Joseph's Hospital, where doctors removed his left eye, which had been lacerated by glass flying from his smashed windshield.

1953

Louis Conrad's schedule on March 21 was not unlike any other day at the self-service gas station he had operated east of the city limits since 1947, when he and his wife moved from Spokane. As he always did, Louis turned off the lights at the front of the station but usually stayed open until midnight. At about 8:30 p.m. a man came to their nearby home seeking Louis and saying that the lights were out. She explained Louis' daily closing ritual. Mrs. Conrad could not identify the man.

Around 10:00 p.m., Louis' wife brought a meal to him at the station and found him dead on the floor by the front window, in which a single bullet hole could be seen. Responding sheriff's officers determined that robbery was the motive, as the cash drawer containing $140 ($1,200) was missing and a $10 bill was found lying in the gravel near one of the gasoline pumps. An autopsy would discover that Louis had been shot twice, with one bullet passing through his heart.

A dark-colored pickup was known to have stopped at the station about 8:30 p.m.

On March 23 and 24, lie detector tests cleared seven suspects in the case. The millpond at Potlatch Forests, Inc. (now Clearwater Paper Company) was lowered by two feet in an attempt to locate the murder weapon, which was determined to be a .38-caliber pistol. They had dragged the pond without results.

Just when police thought the trail had gone cold, they got a break a week later that led to Donald Lee Keeler, Louis' sixteen-year-old nephew who was a junior at Kendrick (Idaho) High School. Keeler had gone on a spending

Above: The Conrad service station, near the old Clearwater dam (*Historic Firsts* 161), at the time of the murder. *Courtesy of the Lewiston Police Department.*

Lef: Louis Conrad. *Courtesy of the Lewiston Police Department.*

Donald Keeler. *Courtesy of the Idaho State Historical Society, AR42 #8630.*

spree that took him to Spokane, where his mother lived. An anonymous tip about a young kid "spending too much money" led to his arrest.

On April 2, officers took Keeler to the gas station, where he reenacted the murder. Police said that Keeler was "cool and composed" as he demonstrated how he fired a shot through the window of the service station, hitting his uncle. When he walked in, Keeler found that Conrad was still alive. When his uncle raised his left arm and cried out, "Oh, no!" Keeler shot him again, this time through the heart. When onlookers got a little too close to the reconstruction, Keeler asked to sit in one of the patrol cars. He waived his right to a preliminary hearing and waited in the county jail for his day of judgment.

On April 22, Keeler pleaded guilty to first-degree murder. Sentencing was delayed when Dr. Robert Wetzler, a Spokane psychiatrist, testified that Keeler was "a simple schizophrenic and was insane when he committed the crime." Judge John Kramer disagreed and said that Keeler's "lack of remorse makes the problem more difficult." He gave Keeler a life sentence. In April 1958, the Idaho Board of Pardons denied his request for clemency but in March 1963 granted him his parole, which he completed in November 1967. On January 13, 1982, Idaho granted Keeler an unconditional pardon and restored "all civil, political, and other rights regardless of kind or character with the same force and effect as if the crime for which this pardon issues had never been committed."

1959

George Kimes was back in jail, this time in Lewiston. Kimes and his brother, Matt, were the core of the infamous Kimes Gang in the 1920s. Woody Guthrie even wrote a song about them. The brothers began at a young age as petty thieves but soon moved on to bank robbery. In August 1926, they robbed two banks in Covington, Oklahoma, within an hour of each other. Two days later, they killed Deputy Sheriff Perry Chuculate in a shootout after being stopped for speeding in a stolen car. Apprehended, the brothers were convicted of manslaughter and sentenced to twenty-five years in prison. George also received a fifty-year sentence for bank robbery. Matt escaped and went on a multi-state crime spree that took four lives. He was sentenced to the electric chair, only to have his sentence commuted.

After thirty years in prison, George was paroled in 1957 and headed to the Northwest. He got into a fight at a Lewiston tavern on December 14, 1959, and stabbed Earl Fish, who recovered and asked that the charges be dropped. In March 1960, prosecuting attorney Owen Knowlton agreed,

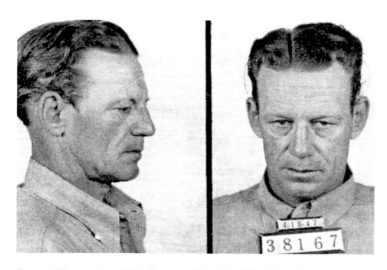

George Kimes, circa 1946. *Courtesy of the Michael Koch Collection.*

citing Kimes' cooperation and the fact that "he appears meek and mild, almost broken by the years." His wife was waiting for him outside the jail, where had spent one hundred days. Of her, he said:

> *She always said she thought there was some good in me, if I could ever get out and have a chance to prove it. I'd rather die than go back* [to prison].

George died in 1970 in California. Matt was killed in December 1945 when a truck struck him.

1963

Charles "Chickie" Berman and his brother, David "Davie the Jew," were gangsters who grew up in Sioux City, Iowa. By the late 1930s, they were the leaders of the Minnesota Mafia. Chickie had been setting up gambling operations while he was serving time in Sing-Sing, the famous New York maximum-security prison. After World War II, the brothers moved to Las Vegas, buying the El Cortez Hotel with several partners in a plan to establish control over the gambling interests in the town. Chickie and Davie teamed up with Benjamin "Bugsy" Siegel to build the Flamingo Hotel.

A compulsive gambler, bookie and snappy dresser, Chickie moved in the mid-1950s to Lewiston, where he took up a new fraud: stock market manipulation. In the meantime, he and his wife began building a new home in the Orchards. In August 1956, they fired the architect of their new house at 540 Grelle. They said that they had wanted only a $35,000 ($300,000) home. Their architect sued, showing that the Bermans wanted a lot more luxury: a three-car garage, a swimming pool, extra baths and a pumice exterior. That pushed the home to half a million dollars in today's values.

In December 1958, Chickie was charged with defrauding investors of $2 million ($16 million) worth of shares in the John Inglis Company of Toronto, Canada, over a three-year period, in what was termed a "boiler room" operation using high-pressure sales tactics.

Those charges did little to deter Chickie's activities. He would sit around in silk robes and constantly be on the telephone with his "contacts." In 1961, an indictment was returned by a grand jury in the Southern District of New York charging thirty-eight individuals and corporations with manipulating

Charles (left) and David Berman, circa 1940. *Courtesy of the Susan Berman Collection.*

the market price of United Dye and Chemical Corporation stock on the New York Stock Exchange. Among the defendants was Charles Berman.

The trial began in March 1962, and in February 1963, Chickie was found guilty. On March 5, he was sentenced to a six-year prison term and a fine of $35,000 ($240,000). He began serving his sentence in February 1964. Total losses to the public in the fraud amounted to $5 million ($36 million). The United Dye case was, at the time, the longest criminal trial in the history of the country's federal courts, lasting eleven months. The court transcript ran to 26,000 pages, and when Judge William Herlands delivered the charge to the jury, his instructions were 450 pages long.

Chickie's story again made front page news in March 2015, when Robert Durst was arrested for the 2000 murder of Susan Berman, Davie's daughter, who lived with Chickie and his wife near the airport after her father died in 1957. Susan attended St. Helen's Hall in Portland, Oregon, for her high school years (*Lost Lewiston* 132–133). According to one source, Chickie did not want to care for a teenager while trying to run his rackets. He died in 1978.

A postscript: In October 1968, the Lewiston City Council approved a payment of $146,000 ($1 million) to the Bermans for the home and eight acres to make room for an expansion of the airport. The house was purchased and moved to Hatwai.

8

WORKS BELONGING TO A DEEP DARKNESS

Cover her face; mine eyes dazzle; she died young.
—John Webster, The Duchess of Malfi

PROLOGUE

The story you are about to read involves a case that is still very raw in the memories of surviving family members. As a historian, I am bound to the truth, but truth need not be brutally presented. No amount of subtlety will totally obscure the violence of murder, but a young mother's life deserves the truth, even if it must be held up for viewing through a filter of sensitivity.

The Rape, Abuse & Incest National Network reports that approximately two-thirds of all sexual assaults are committed by someone known to the victim. About 80 percent of victims are under the age of thirty. At least 98 percent of all rapists will never spend a day in jail. In the case of Jean Johnson, the crime would be doubly disturbing.

Eula Jean Crocker was born on April 27, 1927, in Wallace, Idaho, the daughter of Lester and Nell Crocker. Known to friends and family as Jean, she moved with her parents to Kendrick, Idaho, in 1931. The first mention of her name in print appears in the October 1, 1936 issue of the *Kendrick Gazette*, which reported that she had won first place in the fourth grade division of the district spelling bee. Jean graduated along with my uncle from Kendrick High School in 1944, winning awards in scholarship and bookkeeping. After graduation, she

Jean Johnson, September 28, 1956. *Courtesy of the Lewiston Police Department.*

moved to Palouse, Washington, to work for the Northern Pacific Railroad. On January 7, 1949, she married Richard Johnson. The couple would welcome two daughters—Patricia Ann and Debra Sue—before divorcing in August 1955. Jean took employment at the Lewiston office of the Pacific Telephone and Telegraph Company (PTT) in December, leaving her daughters in the care of her mother during the week. A former telephone company manager, Richard enlisted in the U.S. Navy and was posted to the Philippines.

Jean rented a small studio apartment in an isolated section of the Jess Apartments on the brow of Normal Hill, near Pioneer Park. A local contractor, Henry Jess had the surprisingly ugly Art Deco buildings constructed of fireproof concrete in 1936. They proved popular among newlyweds and young professionals, who could save money by walking to their jobs. Jean's lodgings were a short walk from her work at Sixth Avenue and Sixth Street. To get to her apartment, a visitor had to go down two flights of outside stairs and then walk fifty feet along a ramp that came to an end in brush and barbed wire. Now used only for storage, they are still buildings devoid of any charm.

Described as "a tall, very attractive blonde," Jean no doubt attracted attention as she walked the four blocks from her apartment to work as a clerk at the telephone exchange. Residents of the valley were getting used to dialing seven numbers instead of five. On April 14, the company had instituted the prefixes SHerwood (74 for Lewiston) and PLaza (75 for Clarkston). Gordon

The Jess Apartments, circa 1940. *Courtesy of Amy Campbell.*

Davenport, the regional manager of PTT, commented that her colleagues and superiors thought a great deal of Jean.

Friday, September 28, 1956, looked to be a pleasant day, after a high of sixty-eight degrees Fahrenheit the day before. September can be very hot in Lewiston, with temperatures of one hundred degrees as late as the twenty-fourth. It had been a dry month, but residents anticipated showers that evening and into the weekend. Jean's father would arrive that afternoon to pick her up for the usual thirty-minute drive to Kendrick and her reunion with Patty and Debbie.

When the 8:00 a.m. shift at the telephone exchange began, Jean was unexpectedly absent. She was ever so reliable. By 9:00 a.m., co-worker Della Fix grew concerned. She walked to the apartment building, found Henry Jess and convinced him to open Jean's door. Their discovery launched an investigation that would last thirty years and, based on the evidence, end with a double murder in October 1986.

At first, Della thought that Jean had committed suicide with chloroform. Jean lay dead on her sofa, with a pair of her panties stuffed in her mouth and bruises around her neck. The truth was not so simple. Police chief Frank Hunt mobilized his staff, interviewing more than 130 people, including my maternal grandfather. Investigators found scant evidence in Jean's apartment, which showed no signs of disorder. She had laid out a brown sweater to dry on her table, and her purse sat undisturbed nearby. Burglary was never considered a motive. She knew her assailant. Initially, the police concluded that Jean had been the victim of a sexual assault, but subsequent interviews demonstrated that she was sexually active with two boyfriends.

A crime scene photograph of Jean Johnson's undisturbed purse and sweater. *Courtesy of the Lewiston Police Department.*

Detectives dusted the apartment for prints and found that everything had been wiped clean.

Dr. Donald Merkeley, a Lewiston pathologist, performed the autopsy and declared the cause of death: asphyxia. Her attacker had broken several of her cervical vertebrae, leaving vivid bruising on her neck. Rigor mortis was present only in her fingers. Dr. Merkeley found intense postmortem lividity, a condition where the blood settles to the lowest points in the body, depending on how it is positioned. The violence of her strangulation caused petechiae, the bleeding under the skin commonly seen in strangulation victims, to be found in her eyes, scalp and face. Based on those facts, he determined that Jean had been dead for about six to seven hours when Fix and Jess found her.

The Crockers buried their daughter and sister on October 2 in Lewiston's Normal Hill Cemetery after a service at the local First Methodist Church (*Lost Lewiston* 59), but funerals are not always the same as closure, for the family or investigators who desperately wanted answers for a senseless act.

Police officials recognized almost immediately that Jean's killer was someone whom she willingly let into her apartment. She had returned from a date with John Dunn at about 12:30 a.m. on the morning of her death. Dunn became a prime suspect, along with Vernon Choate, her other suitor. Both voluntarily submitted to and passed polygraph tests, but Choate raised concern among Lewiston and FBI investigators. He was a Kendrick resident and had been dating Jean, although he was a married man passing himself off as single. Jean and Vernon were described as being "recently estranged" at the time of her death. She told a co-worker that she had tired of dating him on the sly.

Clyde Dailey—captain of detectives for the Seattle, Washington Police Department—administered the polygraph. Four questions produced troubling responses from Choate:

Have you told me the truth? Choate answered, *"Yes."*
Were you in Jean's apartment Thursday night? "No."
Did you kill Jean? "No."
Are you concealing any information about the case? "No."

In his report to Lewiston authorities, Dailey concluded, "The test charts contain definite indications of deception, and it is my opinion that Choate was not truthful in answering any of the above questions." Choate claimed that he had not been to Jean's apartment for a few days prior to her death, but crime scene photos show a space heater he told a neighbor he was going to deliver that very evening.

Although the results of the technique cannot be entered as evidence, voice stress analysis records and plots changes in a person's voice when under stress resulting from a question or from what he gives as an answer. The most famous use of the technique was in 2012, when Florida police administered the procedure to George Zimmerman. Choate also underwent the test, and the feedback proved to be very troubling. In his report, the technician who analyzed the data stated that Choate was the most deceptive person he had ever tested and that he may have killed or attempted to kill several times. He would remain the focus of police attention for decades, especially after the case was reopened in 1977.

Vernon choked a new girlfriend, who was in reality a police informant and part of a sting to see if he would confess to Jean's murder. Kendrick's town marshal, Bill White, came upon Choate in an alley with his hands around the throat of another woman. When White challenged Choate, he let the woman go, and she fled. Choate gave White an excuse, but the marshal could never corroborate the alibi, as the woman could not be found later. Vernon had large hands and was not afraid to use them, even on at least one man who crossed him.

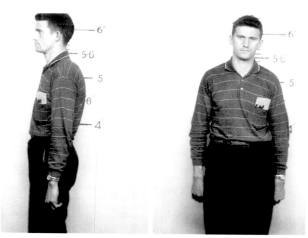

Vernon Choate. *Courtesy of the Lewiston Police Department.*

White would testify that on September 28, 1956, the day Jean's body was found, he and Nez Perce County deputy sheriff Bud Huddleston approached Choate to bring him in for questioning. Vernon asked the officers if the reason for their request was related to the "Jean Johnson deal or murder." As the murder had just been discovered and the officers made no mention of it, how did he know of her death?

Many people have asked, "Why did authorities not charge Vernon with Jean's murder?" Was there not reasonable cause? Certainly, but any competent attorney would raise reasonable doubt in the minds of a jury. A lawyer could easily admit to Choate's abusive and violent personality, how he would burn one of his four wives with cigarette butts and even attempted to drown another in a bathtub after she left him. Vernon Choate exhibited many sociopathic tendencies and became fixated on several women and girls. When caught in a lie soon after Jean's death, he told investigators, "I'll go to prison no matter what I do, so I'd rather not say anything about it. I don't believe it will help me. I'll get hung either way."

Choate's days of philandering, abuse and assaults on women came to an abrupt end on October 12, 1986, nearly thirty years to the day after Jean's murder. He was entertaining a new girlfriend, Mari Martin, who had recently separated from her husband, Raymond. At 9:30 p.m., the two were having a beer with friends at the Bottoms Up Tavern in Juliaetta, a small town three miles west of Kendrick, when Raymond came in very drunk, shouting at Mari and challenging Choate to a fight. Choate tried to calm Raymond by offering to buy him a drink. A reasonable person does not give more alcohol to an inebriated, angry, irrational husband who finds you with his wife. Choate's cunning would be his undoing.

Choate may have thought that he could talk his way out the situation, as he had done so many times before. His ploy seemed to have worked. Raymond left the bar after getting into a shoving match with Mari. He returned about twenty minutes later, pulled out a pistol and shot them both at close range. Choate died immediately from a bullet through his head. Mari died the next day.

All the evidence having been sifted, you must come to your own conclusion. If you were a member of a grand jury, how would you have voted? I can speak for no one but myself. Some Kendrick residents felt Raymond deserved a statue instead of twenty years in the state penitentiary.

Murder may pass unpunish'd for a time, but tardy justice will o'ertake the crime.
—*John Dryden, "The Cock and the Fox"*

9

BETRAYED INNOCENCE
OF THE YOUNG

It is easier to build strong children than to repair broken men.
—*Frederick Douglass*

Violence against children evokes loathing and indignation among adults. Many are surprised to learn that this is so even among hardened criminals. Prisons and jails have their own social classes. Career bank robbers, organized crime bosses and those who kill police officers are treated with the highest levels of deference and respect. On the other hand, inmates who have committed crimes against children, especially sexual abuse, are labeled as "dirty" and undergo harassment and continued abuse by fellow inmates who feel that they are repaying a debt to society by their actions.

Crimes against Lewiston children were not as well reported decades ago as they are today. However, the barrage of media reports can deceive us and skew our perception. Take, for example, the abduction of children, which will be a major part of the discussion to follow. Parents today take great care to instruct their children about the "dangers of strangers." What do the statistics show?

The number of kidnapped children who are taken by strangers constitutes a very small percentage of the reported abductions. Between 1990 and 1995, the National Center for Missing and Exploited Children handled only 515 stranger abductions, a mere 3.1 percent of its caseload.

In a 2000 report issued by the Office of Juvenile Justice and Delinquency Programs, the findings clearly demonstrated that more than three-fourths of abductions were carried out by family members or acquaintances of the child. The study also found that children abducted by strangers were harmed less frequently than those taken by acquaintances. University of Southern California sociology professor Barry Glassner wrote about missing children in his book *The Culture of Fear*:

> *In national surveys conducted in recent years 3 out of 4 parents say they fear that their child will be kidnapped by a stranger. They harbor this anxiety, no doubt, because they keep hearing frightening statistics and stories about perverts snatching children off the street. What the public doesn't hear often or clearly enough is that the majority of missing children are runaways fleeing from physically or emotionally abusive parents.*

With these facts in mind, let us explore some of the news stories that raised righteous anger among Lewiston's citizens.

FRIDAY, JULY 21, 1933, WAS ONE of those very warm summer days that Lewiston so often experiences, and on hot days, children want to play outside. Temperatures were in the nineties, and a sprinkler in the yard would provide all the entertainment any kid could want.

Stanley Goldsmith worked for Gene Mullarky, a prosperous orchardist on Burrell Avenue, near what would later become the regional airport. Stanley's wife, Hazel, worked in the Mullarky home as a housekeeper and cook. The home was also the weather station in the Orchards at the time. The Goldsmiths had lived in the Lewiston Orchards for only a short time, having come from Eugene, Oregon, with their seven children, four of whom were still at home.

At 1:00 p.m., Hazel stepped to the back door of the home to see what her children were doing and witnessed a parent's worst fear. A man was running out of the yard with her youngest child, Virginia Jean, under one arm. Three-year-old Virginia was crying and struggling to free herself. Hazel screamed several times, alerting Stanley, and gave chase. Virginia's writhing was proving to be fruitless.

After carrying the child for about two hundred feet, the man reached Burrell Avenue and turned east. He looked back and saw that Hazel and Stanley were gaining on him and that neighbors were coming out of houses all along the street, reacting to Hazel's loud screams. He dropped Virginia to the dirt road near the intersection with Sixth Street and disappeared. Amid all the hubbub that followed, no one took notice if

The Mullarky home, 1912. *From* Lewiston Orchards Life.

he ran along the road or took off into the nearby orchards that filled the neighborhoods in those days.

Virginia's outcries provoked the assailant to grab her by the throat, the imprint of his fingers leaving blue marks. The *Lewiston Morning Tribune* said, "The man handled the girl severely." Hazel had been so distracted that she could not furnish a description of the man other than that he wore "light overalls that looked like they had been washed" and a cap. A sheriff's posse was quickly organized and searched high and low without success. At first, they suspected that the man was hiding in a nearby clover field. The search continued until late into the afternoon. A door-to-door canvassing failed in an attempt to find anyone who might have seen a stranger. One clue did surface: an unidentified person had slept in the Mullarky packinghouse the previous night.

The sheriff's office and city police reviewed their files and found that a warning had been issued from the state department of corrections to be on the lookout for an escapee from a California insane asylum who was thought to be heading for Idaho. He was described as "dangerous to be at large." Ransom could not have been a factor in Virginia's aborted kidnapping. The Goldsmiths were day laborers. Therefore, the *Tribune* described the event as "the act of a fiend."

On Sunday, July 23, police got their best tip. Charles Sartain came forward after hearing reports of the attempted kidnapping from his wife and son. Sartain was returning to Lewiston from Cottonwood, Idaho, when, about six miles west of Spalding, on the Clearwater River, he came upon a hitchhiker, to whom he gave a lift and dropped off in front of the county courthouse on Main Street, across the street from the train station. During the ride into town, Sartain's passenger "seemed nervous about something." He told Sartain that he was walking from Lapwai but later changed his story to say Arrow Junction. Sartain told police that he could not help noticing the man's "unusual actions."

Sartain's description of his passenger matched that of John Stanovich, who had escaped from the Patton State Hospital in Patton, California, on July 8. The official description matched the man to whom Sartain had given a ride into Lewiston:

> *Age, 45 years; height, five feet seven inches; weight, 145 pounds, black hair; speaks with foreign accent; wearing blue bibless jean overalls, straw hat or cap, no coat, brown shoes like army style, blue work shirt with white stripe.*

This description in hand, police scoured the hobo jungles, but no one answered to the description. Officials began to theorize that Stanovich had cut through the Orchards and followed a winding route to Spalding. From there, he started back to Lewiston, hoping to give himself an alibi for when he arrived in the city. Since that day of turmoil on Burrell Avenue, after which Stanovich most likely hopped aboard a freight train for the coast, Stanovich disappeared from the historical record among the many men with the same name, birth year and foreign origin.

APPEARANCES CAN BE DECEIVING. A case in point occurred at 129 Eighteenth Avenue on February 5, 1915.

In the early morning hours, Prudence Pingree awoke to find a man going out her bedroom door with her three-year-old daughter, Carol, under his arm. Carol had been sleeping in a nearby bed. As Hazel Goldsmith would nearly eighteen years later, Prudence screamed, awaking her husband, Frank, who was sleeping upstairs.

The man dropped Carol and high-tailed it.

When Frank and Prudence searched their home, they found that the intruder had ransacked the house, taking about $18 ($420) in trinkets and cash. The police arrived, took their testimony and started a manhunt, which did not take long. Two men were arrested in a Chinese restaurant downtown.

Officers called Frank to come and identify the crooks, whom he recognized to be men who had been employed at odd jobs around his property. They swiftly confessed, but their intent was not what you think. Carol was not slated to be a kidnap victim. They explained that the child was simply being put somewhere else so her bed could be searched for money that was believed to have been hidden there.

John Strong had lived in the Lewiston area for several years, while his partner and half brother, Robert Lefebvre, had arrived within the previous year. Robert remained outside while John entered the house, which he had cased out. He took his time going through everything before entering Frank's bedroom, where he removed Frank's wallet from his trousers, which were hanging over a chair, emptying it and then replacing it in the pants.

The brothers had been busy and had accumulated a sizeable cache of stolen goods. Earlier in the evening, they had burgled the home of Stephen Taylor, stealing curtains, clothing, utensils, one suit of clothes and, oddly enough, Taylor's false teeth. Judge George Erb set their bond at $2,000 ($47,000) each and whisked them off to the county jail. What had appeared to be a child abduction was just a stupid act by amateur criminals.

RULE NUMBER ONE FOR PARENTS: always vet the people you entrust with the care of your children. To "vet" originally applied to horse racing and referred to the requirement that horses had to be checked by a veterinarian to ensure that they were sound enough to race. In common parlance, it now means "to check or investigate." All too often, people just assume that someone they know will give the same attention and care to their children as they do. The epidemic of live-in boyfriends who abuse, maim or kill children belies that assumption. A case in point occurred in Lewiston in February 1897.

At some point previous to that date, Isabelle Hagen had left her two sons, ages five and seven, in the care of her husband's brother while she went out to seek employment. She also started divorce proceedings against her husband, Arnold, who was in an Oregon hospital, presumably a mental institution. This action angered her brother-in-law, and he refused to continue to care for the boys.

Without informing Isabelle, he took the boys to an isolated site on the Camas Prairie and left them in a deserted building without provisions. The next morning, Thomas Stevens found the children, by that time numb with cold and very frightened. Stevens warmed and fed them, returning them

South Snake River Avenue, circa 1918. *Courtesy of the Vaden Floch Archives.*

to Lewiston after questioning the boys about where they had been living. Probate judge Prince Stookey returned the children to relatives who would give the boys proper care.

We are left with nagging questions without solutions. Did Isabelle ever reclaim her boys? And what did officials do about her uncaring brother-in-law?

ONE OF LEWISTON'S MOST DISTURBING and mysterious child death cases occurred in April 1913. A passerby discovered the bodies of two infants hidden under the old board sidewalk on South Snake River Avenue. The investigating officers reported that each child had been wrapped in a blanket. Physicians determined that the boy and girl were twins and only a day or two old at the time of their deaths. If this was a case of birth complications, why were the bodies hidden? Where the infants alive when they were placed under the sidewalk?

Several theories are possible, but one seems more likely than the rest: an unwed mother was concealing a tragic end to an unwanted pregnancy.

BEFORE LEAVING THE TOPIC of abandonment, here is a story of Lewiston's first foundling, at least from what Lewiston's old-timers could remember. Jim Conley arrived with his mother in 1867, and he could not recall another case.

On the morning of February 3, 1941, sixty-two-year-old bachelor Ben Callison stepped onto the porch of his home at 212 Eighteenth Avenue and found something other than his *Lewiston Morning Tribune*. It was a crying baby boy. Ben gave a good account of what happened:

> *I was awakened about 5:15 by what I thought was the whining of a puppy at my back door. I went to the back door and found no trace of a puppy. I went to the front door and found the blue-eyed boy in a clothes basket. I didn't know what to do.*

Composing himself, Ben brought the basket into the house, put on some clothes and went next door to the home of Alvin and Frances Gwynne, who had two children of their own. Frances unwrapped the baby and warmed some milk for him, which quelled his crying as she called the police station. Callison had no idea where the child came from. In 1941, Eighteenth Avenue was the last street with residences on the southwestern edge of the city. Having heard no noise of a car, Ben thought that the child must have been "carried from the country road" one block south of his home. That "country road" is now Southway, a main east–west arterial. Police officers found tire tracks indicating that a car had stopped on the road below Callison's home.

Someone abandoned the baby boy in an ordinary woven clothes basket and wrapped it in a large blue and white blanket to ward off the cold of the February morning. He wore a "snuggle-bunny" fitted with a hood. Alongside the basket, Ben found seven clean diapers, two new baby sweaters and two new baby shirts. Because the milk in his bottle was still warm, Callison guessed that the boy had been on his porch for a very short time.

Police chief Eugene Gasser notified the public nurse and the Red Cross, who arrived to take custody of the child and have the boy checked out by the staff at St. Joseph's Hospital. Judge John Phillips then took the case under advisement pending further investigation.

Applications to adopt the three-month-old child came flooding in. By the next day, Phillips had more than thirty petitions on his desk. All the while, baby Lewis Clark, as the nurses were calling him, became a favorite among the staff. Happy and contented, he would coo in his crib, alternating between sucking his thumb and smiling.

The community opened its arms and heart to the boy. Businesses even offered jobs to the mother if she would just come forward. There are no reports of that happening. The search for the mother grew cold, and the boy disappeared into the anonymity of Idaho's adoption program.

History repeated itself when a day-old baby boy was abandoned on April 7, 1963, on the porch of Helen Ingle's home at 908 Eighth Avenue. "I was shook up," Ingle related after finding the boy when she went for her morning paper. The police were called, and the baby rode in a police cruiser to St. Joseph's Hospital for observation. The nuns at the hospital named him Joseph Saturday, for the hospital and the day of the week when he was found. Unlike the child found on Callison's porch, Joseph's mother came forward. In her early thirties and divorced, she had delivered the child alone in a bedroom while her other six children were watching television.

Carrying the baby in a cardboard box, she started for the hospital but became too tired to walk any farther when she reached Ingle's residence. "I want to have my baby back if I can have him without giving up my other children," she testified in a custody hearing on May 6. She was worried that the court would take her children away if officials learned that she had another baby while unmarried. Since the boy was found, thirty-five couples had offered to adopt Joseph.

FREDERICK WEYERHAEUSER, THE HEAD of the largest timber syndicate in the United States, visited Lewiston in 1902 to survey the Leslie Porter property east of the city (*Historic Firsts* 111). The previous winter, Weyerhaeuser had expressed the intention of placing a large lumber mill on the site. His private automobile came on the train with him for his use around Lewiston. Although Weyerhaeuser told city officials that his company had "secured a site for a sawmill," he could not state when the work would begin. Little did anyone realize at the time that more than twenty years would pass before it started.

On April 13, 1925, the city council accepted the proposal of the Clearwater Timber Company and the Inland Power and Light Company in the matter of establishing mills along the Clearwater River east of town. The city committed itself to "securing sites at reasonable prices," and the companies agreed to have the plants in operation by the summer of 1927, a deadline that the companies met. The initial investments of the two companies were estimated to total $4.5 million ($60 million).

But what does this have to do with crimes against Lewiston children?

The story line to a tale that captivated the nation begins when Frederick's grandson John Phillip Weyerhaeuser Jr. moved his wife, Helen, and their two small sons, John III and George, to Lewiston when he was appointed the general manager of Clearwater Timber in 1927. Sadly, their three-month-old son Frederick died on February 7, 1928. That fall, the Weyerhaeusers moved into what many call "the Potlatch House" on Sixth Avenue. The

John and Helen Weyerhaeuser, 1935. *Courtesy of the Tacoma Public Library, 2500-5.*

Clearwater Timber Company, the Edward Rutledge Timber Company (Coeur d'Alene) and the Potlatch Lumber Company merged in May 1931 to create Potlatch Forest, Inc., with John as its first president. His next corporate move took the family to Tacoma, Washington, in 1933, when John became executive vice-president of Weyerhaeuser Timber.

Few families rode out the Great Depression more successfully than the Weyerhausers, but in May 1935, John and Helen's gilded life came to a screeching halt. On May 24, son George, now nine years old, left the upscale Lowell School he attended to meet his sister Ann, who was a student at Annie Wright Seminary, in the North End neighborhood of Tacoma. As George was let out early for lunch, he decided to walk home by himself. On any other day, the family chauffeur would meet the children at the seminary. John and Helen searched for him. Maybe he just stopped by the home of a classmate. The truth became apparent that evening when a ransom note, addressed "To Whom It May Concern," arrived by special delivery at the family home. Among the demands was the payment of $200,000 ($4.5 million) in unmarked small bills—twenties, tens and fives. The kidnappers had George sign his name on the back of the envelope to confirm that they had him.

George Weyerhaeuser, 1935. *Courtesy of the Tacoma Public Library, 2500-61A.*

The Weyerhaeusers placed notes in the *Seattle Post-Intelligencer* to indicate that they had received the kidnappers' instructions and were ready to comply. On May 29, John checked into the Ambassador Hotel and awaited word. His next orders instructed him to follow a trail of stakes with pieces of signal cloth attached. The kidnappers failed to leave a note at the final stop in John's search, and that set the process back to square one. The next evening, John parked his car on a side road between Seattle and Tacoma, left the money in the seat and starting walking back toward Seattle. He had not walked very far when he heard someone start the car and drive off.

While all the arrangements were underway to drop the ransom money, the kidnappers were moving George around, in part to keep him from identifying landmarks and in part to elude the police and FBI. They even dug a large hole and hid him in it, chaining his right wrist and leg together. The kidnappers drove George as far as Blanchard, Idaho, in the panhandle of the state. He was finally left in a small building near Issaquah, Washington, east of Seattle, in the early morning hours of June 1.

It did not take long for the kidnappers to mess up. All of the serial numbers on the ransom money had been recorded. When bills began appearing in Salt Lake City, the FBI zeroed in. On June 19, 1935, a federal grand jury in Tacoma returned an indictment charging William Dainard, Harmon Waley and Margaret Waley with kidnapping and conspiracy to kidnap. Agents recovered $157,319.47 from the ransom money and funds that had been exchanged by the kidnappers to keep the bills from being traced. Armed with fingerprint evidence and confessions, the United States District Court handed down sentences ranging from twenty to sixty years for the caper.

George would return to school, grow up and graduate from Yale in 1948. Working his way from a mill foreman, he became the president of Weyerhaeuser in 1966 and was a director of the Boeing Company. In a final twist, when Harmon Whaley earned his parole from the McNeil Island Penitentiary in June 1963, he was the last of the kidnappers to be released from custody. Harmon wrote to George several times over the years, repeatedly apologizing for his role on the events. Upon his release, he asked George for a job and was given employment at a company plant in Oregon.

To complete this chapter, let us explore how Lewiston has responded to the welfare of children, as well as to juvenile mischief and delinquency, boredom and chicanery.

When residents organized the Lewiston Library Association in the late 1870s, the purpose of the new collection had young people in mind, as reported in the January 22, 1878 issue of the *Lewiston Teller*:

> *Our citizens should see to it that the library room should be well supplied with reading matter, and kept open as a place of resort for our young people where they can make mental progress and be directed from those influences that are demoralizing.*

Not every child could or wanted to read.

At the October 3, 1892 meeting of the city council, mayor Charles Kress called attention to how boys were "depredating" (laying waste to, plundering) on city streets at night. Passed on October 6, 1883, Ordinance 66 had prohibited boys from being on the streets after certain hours. Until 1888, the local school had an organized curriculum only to the eighth grade, so young boys had a lot of time on their hands after the age of fourteen. Kress brought up the matter again on December 5. He was getting too much heat from residents.

City officials did what they could to encourage healthy activities to get kids off the streets. In December 1893, the council opened its meeting room at city hall to the "juvenile band" so it could have a place to practice. Lewiston was a dirty town that had no parks or community centers.

The city also acted to protect the health of children. On November 6, 1899, the council responded to an outbreak of smallpox, recommending that public schools be closed for thirty days and that parents keep their children off the streets. The town marshal was ordered to arrest any child under fifteen years old found in the street for the next month. All public meetings—including lodge, churches and amusement—were prohibited.

In June 1900, the city council granted a local man the right to remove dead animals from city streets. That nuisance abated, the council followed up in August by forbidding the riding of bicycles and tricycles on sidewalks. Lewiston's kids were getting some attention, but not the kind they wanted.

A group of concerned citizens petitioned the city in April 1906 to appoint a probation officer. So many cases of crime had been reported among young boys that people were convinced that adults had to be "leading the young astray." A probation officer could corral the instigators and protect the young boys and girls.

A "gang" was already known to exist in the town. Composed of about twenty-six individuals, the group used the stage of the local theater during the evening hours. Although most of the gang members were young, at least one married man associated regularly. The kids always had liquor, but no one would "rat out" the person who was supplying it. The police had been keeping an eye on the gatherings and had identified about a dozen criminals who frequented the "dances" held by the teenagers.

Speaking for himself and other Lewiston pastors, Reverend William Euster (*Lost Lewiston* 57–59) was not shy in his opinion of what should be done with the ringleaders and what the effects on the town would be if the city council did not act. "When once the hand of the law has taken them in tow and they are prosecuted and sent to prison, then the payday comes in increased taxes," he said. The ministers implored the council to focus attention on those children who could be helped and send "those who are really going down to crime" to the Idaho Industrial Reform School in St. Anthony, a small isolated town west of Grand Teton National Park.

The recommendation for a probation officer found favor. The August 4, 1908 issue of the *Spokane (WA) Spokesman-Review* reported that the parents of Bertha Molloy had turned her over to the officer. A repeat runaway, Bertha received a sentence to serve a term in the reform school for incorrigibility. Bernice McCoy, then the county superintendent of schools, escorted Bertha to St. Anthony. The reformatory had a troubling reputation. In August 1912, a sensational scandal erupted. Testimony at a formal investigation of the school indicated that boys were being stripped of their clothing and lashed with heavy straps. Four such straps were entered as evidence, along with accounts of their being used for child beatings. As a boy, I know that just the threat of being sent to St. Anthony put the fear of God in us. Today, the facility is known as the Idaho Juvenile Corrections Center.

North Idaho Children's Home, 1914. *Courtesy of Special Collections and Archives, University of Idaho Library, 09-15-03a.*

In the fall of 1908, Samuel Chase and his wife began taking homeless children into their care. After joining with the Boise-based Children's Home Finding and Aid Society of Idaho, they organized what would become the Northwest Children's Home. By 1910, a building had to be rented to satisfy the needs of a growing population. The Chases' success filled the building. On March 11, 1912, the Children's Home governing board signed the papers to buy the Hurlbut home in Blanchard Heights. The state pledged $7,000 ($170,000) toward the purchase, and the remaining $7,000 was raised in pledges from individuals, organizations and most of Idaho's ten northern counties. The deed was finalized in December 1913. Additional buildings were constructed over the years. In 1935, the organization became the Children's Home Finding and Aid Society of North Idaho but continued to be known in northern Idaho simply as the Children's Home.

Lewiston's first Boy Scout troop was fully organized and functioning by early 1911. National records from the period are very sparse. The group was certainly north Idaho's, if not the state's, first troop.

In the meantime, organized baseball had taken hold in Lewiston (*Historic Firsts* 124–125), but local boys were not too happy with the

The children's play *Pantomime Cinderella*, 1895. The child playing Cupid was Ermeth Louise McConville (1888–1990), the daughter of Edward McConville (*Historic Firsts* 101–102). *Courtesy of the Nez Perce County Historical Society.*

school board in December 1912. For some unknown reason, boys could no longer play football on any school campus on Sunday.

It took concerned parents to build the first public school in 1872. Parents and grandparents again and again passed bond elections. John and Sarah Vollmer left millions of dollars in today's values and property for "a public building for the use of children in the way of swimming pools and equipment." That initiative eventually became what is now Fenton Park (originally Vollmer Park) and the Bert Lipps municipal pool. In June 1945, Lewiston became the site of Idaho's first boys' club (*Historic Firsts* 147–149).

No one can deny many Lewiston residents genuinely tried to mold its youth for the better, but as a whole, the town did not practice what it preached.

10

FOOL ME ONCE, SHAME ON YOU

Whoever is detected in a shameful fraud is ever after not believed
even if they speak the truth.
—Phaedrus

On not a few occasions, Lewiston's laissez-faire mindset has embraced or rallied around residents convicted of serious crimes (*Hidden History* 76–78). This is a story of an outrageous scheme whose chutzpah baffled even a United States president and probably made him doubt the intelligence of the town's citizens. It is a story with all the twists and turns of a Six Flags Over Texas rollercoaster.

Isaac Newton Hibbs was born in Carthage, Illinois, on March 10, 1851, to James and Elizabeth Hibbs, whose brood numbered six sons and a daughter by 1870. The family had moved west in 1862 over the Oregon Trail. On that trip by oxen team, Newton, as his family called him, had his first experiences hunting wild game and fishing in virgin waters. With the great abundance of wildlife available along the trek, he became an expert with a rifle and rod before his family reached Yamhill County, Oregon. Newton took up farming and stock raising when he reached an age to venture out on his own.

Yamhill County had a serious problem: it was located on a major migratory route for geese and ducks. So many fowl came to the valley that farmers were hard-pressed to save their wheat crops. Seizing the opportunity, Hibbs supplemented his income by shooting birds, as well as hunting big

Isaac Newton Hibbs, 1895. *From* Recreation, *April 1895.*

game animals. On April 23, 1874, he married Ella A. Roberts, a native Oregon girl, in McMinnville.

By 1877, Newton and Ella were a familiar sight on the streets of Lewiston, and he seems to have quickly developed a good reputation among his fellow Lewistonians. On November 2, 1880, they elected him to the House of Representatives of the Eleventh Idaho Territorial Legislature as a Republican. Of note is the fact that it was this legislature that chartered the Lewiston school district (*Historic Firsts* 71–73).

Hibbs served one term and would soon be on to his next public office.

Before 1912, Lewiston had no federal building in which to house the United States Post Office. Buildings along Main Street served that purpose (*Lost Lewiston* 41). Postmasters, who were local businessmen, performed their duties from a space inside their stores dedicated to post office business. In the first Sanborn map of Lewiston, dated March 1888, the post office was housed in the jewelry store of Charles Kress, across the street from the Grostein and Binnard Grand Opera House (*Historic Firsts* 73). Kress will reenter this story later.

Newton Hibbs received his congressional appointment as Lewiston's postmaster on January 18, 1884, succeeding Warren Hunt (*Lost Lewiston* 136), who had held the title since October 1877. Hunt owned a stage and express delivery line, while also serving as the county recorder and auditor.

No records give the location of the Hibbs post office. The limited biographical data gleaned from his later years do not mention that he followed any specific trade. If he was still engaged in stock raising, he may or may not have had an office in town. With that in mind, he may have used an office at the old Nez Perce County Courthouse at Third and C Streets, which was the former Luna House Hotel and had many rooms for use. Lewiston's first post office in July 1862 also found room in the county courthouse, which was then on First Street and included a jail. If Hibbs did rent space in the courthouse, it would have been a prophetic choice. He would be housed in the building under different circumstances the next year, but that fact is a little ahead of our story.

The office of postmaster required more than just an appointment. As a federal official, Newton was required to post a substantial bond. His considerable stature in the community convinced five local leaders—William F. Kettenbach, John Evans, Joseph Alexander (*Lost Lewiston* 37), Ray Woodworth and Johan D.C. Thiessen (*Lost Lewiston* 24–25)—to step up, each posting a $4,000 ($105,000) bond on February 1 to underwrite Hibbs' worthiness and fidelity. In two years, these would be five very unhappy men. Maybe they should have read their newspapers more closely.

Silver City is situated in Owyhee County, in southern Idaho, and was a major town in pre-statehood days, having been the site of the first daily newspaper and the first telegraph office in the territory. On June 6, 1870, Rufus King became the postmaster of the booming community. Beginning in 1864, people could purchase and send money orders, buying them at their local post offices. Problems began to arise, and in 1872, Congress enacted the Mail Fraud Statute. The new law reaped some early fruit.

Silver City had been a town flushed with money, but the passage of the Mint Act in February 1873 literally changed its fortunes. Silver prices

William Kettenbach, 1890. *Courtesy of the City of Portland, Oregon Archives.*

plummeted, and the lucrative Owyhee placer mines began to fail. With his private business no doubt suffering, King aspired to earn some dishonest gain. He proceeded to forge money orders to the tune of about $6,000 ($120,000) and had them cashed in the East. Realizing that his embezzlement scheme was about to be unmasked, he fled to Ogden, Utah, where officials caught up with him on April 18. He was extradited in late May, stood trial in Idaho and sent off to the state penitentiary. Audacious crimes are often pulled off by taking advantage of people's inattention (*Lost Lewiston* 11–12). Newton Hibbs was paying attention.

In January 1885, the registered mail pouch bound for Lewiston from Dayton, Washington, was rifled. The official investigation produced no findings. Among other things, that pouch contained a new supply of money order forms for the postmaster. Those money orders were worth more than $400 ($11,000). People in Lewiston forgot about the missing bag. The United States Post Office did not, and veteran inspector John Murphy dug his teeth into the case like a stubborn bulldog.

In early 1885, no one in Lewiston had thought it unusual to see their postmaster waving goodbye to his wife and young daughter as their riverboat cast off at the Snake River landing on the end of B Street. Ella was going for a visit to McMinville. Newton needed to think. The postal inspector for Idaho had his suspicions that the pouch had been stolen at the Lewiston post office and recommended that Hibbs should not be allowed any credit and the loss charged against him. As a result, in April, Hibbs was suspended as postmaster, and it was in the period between his removal and the naming of Charles Kress as his successor that he did his greatest damage to the postal money order system in the United States.

John Murphy, circa 1905. *From* History of the Bench and Bar in Oregon *(1910)*.

With his family safely away, Hibbs was ready to put the final stage of his plan into action. The effects of his fraud would force the federal government to reorganize its money order system in the United States and abroad. Newspapers across the country later quoted post office officials as saying they were "surprised that it was never thought of or worked before."

Hibbs' modus operandi was surprisingly simple. Lewiston was the distribution point for a large number of post offices in northern Idaho and eastern Washington. Newton would issue a money order listing the name of a post office in his region and under a fictitious name, usually "John G. Wilson" or "J.G. Wilson." The money order was then sent to banks back East. Several were traced to Decatur, Illinois. Hibbs would then write a letter to the paying postmaster, asking him to cash the money order and place the funds in a local bank until he arrived to pick up the funds. At this point, Newton inserted his own twist into the scheme that King had failed to use in 1873.

After a week or so, he would write to his fellow postmaster to say that he was unable to make his planned visit and requested that the postmaster send the money by registered mail addressed to the same person he had falsified in the money order. When the bank drafts arrived, Hibbs signed the receipt card with his alias, returned the card and the transaction was complete. He limited the money orders to $300 ($7,800) and judiciously spread the fraudulent money orders among the post offices whose mail passed over his desk. Between April 1, 1884, and May 1, 1885, he wrote phony money orders totaling $20,645.28 ($550,000). Whether someone began asking questions, we do not know. Suffice it to say, Newton packed up and lit out on May 2, telling people that he was going to check on some mining investments he had made in Canada. At least part of that story was the truth.

Passing himself off as a cattle dealer named T.G. Wilson, he soon showed up in Little Dalles, Oregon, on the Lower Columbia River east of Portland, telling people that he was about to enter into a contract with the Canadian Pacific Railway Company. The *Daily British Colonist* of July 1, 1885, picks up the story:

He gave it to be understood that he had made a large sum of money in the cattle business, making no secret of the fact that he had lived for some years at Lewiston. Owing to some delay in the departure of the steamboat [Kootenai], Hibbs was compelled to wait several days in the Little Dalles, but he seemed to evince no anxiety about this, and had no apparent desire to get across "the line" into the haven for defaulting bank cashiers. While in the Little Dalles someone recognized him, and surprised to see him so far from home said, "Hello, Hibbs, what brings you out here?" Hibbs looked at his questioner, and replied with the greatest nonchalance that his name was not Hibbs and said he had not had the pleasure of meeting him before. Throughout his stay in the Little Dalles, Hibbs kept up his assumed character of a wealthy stockman to perfection, and no one had the remotest idea that he was the gentleman whom the police were so anxiously inquiring after. Perhaps one of the chief reasons accounting for the man's apparent security was the fact that the Little Dalles is two days' journey from any point of telegraphic communication, and is only a few miles from the boundary border.

He arrived in Victoria, British Columbia, on May 25 and registered at the new Oriental Hotel, one of the first built in Old Town, under the name John G. Wilson. His stay in the provincial capital was cut short. George L. Seybolt, chief postal inspector for the Pacific Coast, quickly grew suspicious when his queries to the Lewiston post office were going unanswered. Hibbs' downfall was his telling his Lewiston neighbors that he was going to Canada. Upon learning this, Seybolt dispatched Murphy and a colleague named Culver to Victoria to coordinate their efforts with the British Columbia Provincial Police. Newton expected a large amount of cash to reach him in Victoria, but the American consulate had already persuaded Canadian postal officials not to deliver anything to him under his aliases.

Frederick Hussey, circa 1893. *Courtesy of the Royal British Columbia Museum and Archives, G-09546.*

The provincial police swung into action, assigning Constable Frederick Hussey to head up the case. American investigators had no authority to arrest Hibbs. Hussey would rise through the ranks with special assignments like this one, finally being promoted to superintendent commanding the provincial police in 1891. He would begin his search in the city. The game was afoot. Hibbs paid the bill at the hotel and dropped out of sight for a few days.

Newton checked back into the Oriental on June 2, this time with Ella and Grace, and then left a few days later for the interior of the province just one day ahead of his Canadian and American pursuers, leaving his family in Victoria. He traveled up the Fraser River and then set out for Farwell (now Revelstoke), on the Columbia River and some four hundred miles east of Vancouver. On the trip up the Fraser, Hibbs struck up friendships with several of the passengers and was very generous with his money, even volunteering a loan of a couple thousand dollars to one man, telling him that he did not need any security. Just when this story could not get any weirder, a Lewiston banker showed up.

Wiliam Kettenbach, the president of the Lewiston National Bank, which in 1885 was located at the corner of First and Main Streets, was also hot on Newton's heels. Kettenbach wanted his bond money back before the government had a chance to seize it, and he would be able to identify the runaway postmaster to the police. Although there was little friendship among them, Kettenbach and the two American agents decided to work together under Hussey's leadership to apprehend Newton, who was laying out $3,000 ($80,000) to build a new hotel in Farwell. Almost immediately upon arriving in the new town, Newton was recognized by a Lewiston resident named Allen. Finding it impossible to hide his identity, he admitted that he was traveling under the alias of Wilson and begged Allen "not to give him away." Hibbs knew that the authorities were looking for him. His story was featured in the newspapers, but he had no idea the police and post office detectives were so close. He had ordered furniture for the hotel and was on his way back to Victoria to buy provisions for his new business.

Hussey, Murphy, Culver and Kettenbach finally caught up with Hibbs on June 16 at Harrison River (now Harrison Mills). Hussey arrested Newton and took him to the town of Yale, where the party stayed in the same hotel a few days before, the agents having not recognized Hibbs, as Kettenbach had been busy with other affairs. When Hussey searched Newton, he found his

Bastion Square prison, Victoria, British Columbia, circa 1879. *Courtesy of the Victoria, BC Police Historical Society.*

clothes to be literally padded with bank notes: $500s, $100s and $50s, to the amount of $10,500 ($275,000). That would just cover Kettebach's bond, but the money was Queen's evidence.

While he was in Farwell, he had dropped $200 ($5,400) in a card game with a professional gambler, who, when later learning that Hibbs had more than $10,000 on his person, told investigators that he was almost tempted to commit suicide. He had let a plump pigeon get away.

Hibbs confessed to having written the phony money orders with fictitious names but resisted the claim that he had committed forgery, something he said he "was careful not to do." It would take a federal court to decide the issue, but more about that later.

Agent Hussey, Hibbs now in tow, boarded the steamer *Yosemite* and headed down the Fraser River for the coast and the provincial prison in Victoria. Hussey delivered Hibbs to the Bastion Square facility on June 23. Ella and Grace were waiting. Newton would stay under guard in the Victoria "police barracks" in Bastion Square for one month before the wheels of justice began to turn. On July 27 and July 29, Murphy made his case for extradition before Henry Crease, chief justice of the British Columbia Supreme Court, citing thirty-nine counts of "forging and uttering" post money orders.

According to Justice Crease, the Hibbs case "called for very close attention." The hearings produced volumes of information from American and Canadian sources. The sessions disclosed that Hibbs had also used the alias "W.H. Dent," but the litigation focused on the "definition of forgery

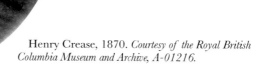

Henry Crease, 1870. *Courtesy of the Royal British Columbia Museum and Archive, A-01216.*

under our criminal law." In a lengthy and detailed decision forwarded to Ottawa, Crease found that that Hibbs' scheme was "a deliberate case of wholesale forgery and breach of trust." In an effort to convince federal officials that extradition was appropriate, he wrote that the action "would be notice everywhere that the skillfully planned postal frauds are powerless before the prompt and vigorous administration of the law."

Canadian lawyers weighed their options until September 10, when Minister of Justice Alexander Campbell issued a warrant for Hibbs'

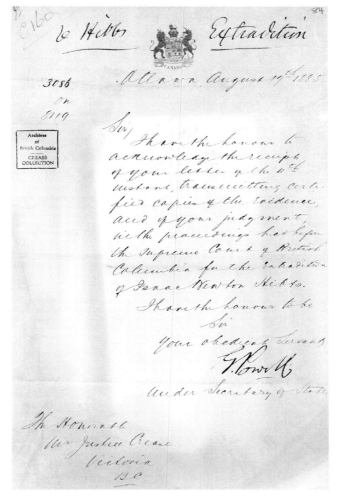

Acknowledgment of the extradition order (cover). *Courtesy of the Royal British Columbia Museum and Archives, MS-55, Box 2, File 9, Item 84.*

extradition to the United States, remanding him into John Murphy's custody. Hibbs had spent seventy-nine days in the provincial prison. The Canadian police chained a twenty-pound steel ball to his leg until Hibbs was safely in the hands of American officials and aboard a ship bound for the United States. Newton would have more opportunities to become accustomed to hoosegow chow.

Murphy took Hibbs to Salem, Oregon, to await the district court's session in Lewiston, where a grand jury indicted him on four counts of forgery on November 20 and ordered that he be remanded in the Nez Perce County jail. Newton had been in one jail or another for five months. Although having admitted to the crimes, he pleaded "not guilty" on December 8, and his trial began the next day.

Despite overwhelming evidence to the contrary, the jury returned a verdict of "not guilty" on the sixteenth. Jurors could not agree on a verdict on one count, so the judge dismissed the jury but put Hibbs back into custody. There were many more charges pending, but the government did not know if a Lewiston jury would ever convict Newton.

At this point, Augustus Garland, attorney general of the United States, took matters into his own hands and contacted Norman Buck, associate justice of the

Norman Buck (standing second from left), 1859. *Courtesy of the Lawrence University Archives, ARC2014-065.*

Idaho Supreme Court. A Lewiston resident (*Historic Firsts* 80–81), Buck issued a bench warrant on December 21 to Fred Dubois, the United States marshal for Lewiston's judicial district, to convey Hibbs to the territorial prison in Boise. Dubois had visited Hibbs in the Bastion Square facility in July 1885 and now made the case that the county jail in Lewiston was not secure. Newton would be housed in Boise for "safe-keeping." There was a hitch in this plan: the only route to Boise in those days took Dubois and Hibbs into Oregon.

Fred Dubois, circa 1895. *Courtesy of the United States Senate Historical Office.*

Unknown to Hibbs, his attorneys and Ella got wind of what was going on and successfully obtained a writ of habeas corpus from the U.S. District Court in Oregon. Dubois had to deliver Hibbs to Oregon authorities and show just cause for his "capture and retention." The proceedings stalled Dubois and Judge Buck's plans until February 1886, when the Oregon court ruled that "the prisoner must be remanded to the custody of the marshal of Idaho, whence he was taken" and clarified that Hibbs had indeed perpetrated forgery. Newton headed to his third confinement and awaited another trial.

Although the American courts were catching up with Newton, the legal wrangling continued over the proceedings in Victoria. The United States government had retained Canadian attorneys, at $1,000 ($26,000) for each lawyer. When, in January 1886, the bill came in, the U.S. Treasury objected and denied the claim. The January 8, 1886 issue of the *Victoria Daily Colonist* commented:

> *There is no doubt, however, that the Victoria lawyers will get their money, for even the treasury officials hold out in the belief that Congress will naturally appropriate the sum necessary to pay for such services, Congress is seldom niggardly in matters of the kind.*

Dubois delivered Newton back to Lewiston in the fall of 1886 for his second trial. Indicted this time on eight more counts, he would not be as lucky. While the jury could not agree on four counts, it did find him guilty on the other four. In January 1887, that was more than enough to earn him a sentence of five years in the state penitentiary. In the meantime, the December 31, 1886 issue of the *Willamette Farmer* quipped that "the [Victoria] lawyers will probably get the rest of the 'boodle.'"

The trek to justice seemed to be done, but not so fast. The new postmaster, Charles Kress, had called in Hibbs' bond on February 27, 1886. When Alexander, Kettenbach and the others resolutely refused to pay, the United States district attorney, James Hawley (who became Idaho's governor from 1911 to 1913), finally filed a lawsuit in August 1888 to recover $10,000. Convinced by district attorney Alfred Quackenbush's arguments, the jury decided in the government's favor on November 24. The bondsmen's attorney? Norman Buck, who had recently returned to private practice and would become a member of the Washington State Supreme Court in 1892.

Undeterred, Hibbs' allies tried another tactic. Buck and Quackenbush petitioned President Grover Cleveland for a pardon. Cleveland would have none of it and on February 16, 1889, wrote:

> *I cannot agree with the judge* [Buck] *and district attorney* [Quackenbush] *in their recommendation for a pardon in this case. The convict's offense was as deliberately planned and executed as possible, so that he has no sudden temptation to plead. He took advantage of the position of trust he held to rob the Government. His good standing gained him the position, and having used that good character indirectly to betray his trust, it should be of little avail to him now. He fled from justice and yielded no right which he could interpose to the cause of justice, and at every step added to the public exposure and loss. I am not insensible to the appeal to sympathy presented by the distress of his wife and family, and the disgrace of friends, but the performance of pubic duty must not yield to such considerations. This is emphatically the case, in my opinion, to which Executive clemency should not be extended.*

Why had Buck and Quackenbush bypassed territorial governor Edward Stevenson? The reason becomes vividly apparent after reading a letter written not long before by the district attorney of Kootenai County, when Judge Buck recommended the pardon of Charles Ross, who had been convicted of manslaughter in 1887:

> *I do not believe it will have any effect on the Governor. First, because Governor Stevenson will not pardon Ross if every man in the Territory recommended it*

Above: Nez Perce County Courthouse, circa 1885. *Courtesy of the Nez Perce County Historical Society.*

Right: James Hawley, circa 1910. *Courtesy of the Library of Congress.*

unless he is convinced that it was justifiable homicide, and secondly, that Judge Buck has never convinced Gov. Stevenson of his ability, honesty, or fairness any more than he has the people of Kootenai or Shoshone Counties, and I can just fancy Gov. Stevenson throwing down his recommendation with a look of disgust and the forcible remark of "Judge Buck be damned."

Buck and Quackenbush seem to have forgotten that Cleveland had just used his pocket veto in March 1887, as a favor to Stevenson, to derail the bill to carve out north Idaho off from the rest of the territory.

Hibbs' bondsmen appealed to the Ninth District Court of Appeals in 1892, getting the same answer: pay up. In his ruling for the government, Justice Matthew Paul Deady gave a blunt review, "It would be a reproach to the law of this country if the prisoner could not be punished for his misconduct while acting as postmaster of Lewiston."

Newton was not wasting his time while a prison inmate. He had been publishing poetry in *The West Shore* magazine since April 1888. He wrote the chapter "Moose-Hunting in the Rocky Mountains" for the 1890 volume *Big Game of North America*, which also lists him as "Roxey Newton," his nom de plume. He knew a lot about aliases.

A little math tells us that Newton had been released from prison by the fall of 1893. His second daughter, Alta, was born in August 1894. The October 1895 issue of *Recreation* magazine featured him as one of its contributors. The editors noted that he had been "appointed postmaster at Lewiston, by President Arthur, a position he held for many years." Hibbs would not be the last person to pad his resumé and smooth over his failings.

Hibbs came close to drowning on May 21, 1897, when a ferry on which he was a passenger sank between Lewiston and what is now Clarkston, Washington. The ferry was overloaded with cattle. One man died.

The Hibbs family left Lewiston for good in 1902 for a home on the Salmon River. Newton had developed a new career as a mining expert, joining other Lewiston businessmen to form a mining exchange in November 1899. After living in Salmon and Twin Falls, Idaho, for several years, Newton and Ella moved to Evanston, Wyoming, to spend their last years with their daughter Alta and her family. Having outlived Murphy, Kettenbach, Buck, Crease and Dubois, Newton passed away on September 25, 1935, a widely respected old man whose past had long since been put behind him. He had not tried fooling people twice.

11

SHE'S COME UNDONE

Heaven has no rage like love to hatred turned, nor hell a fury
like a woman scorned.
—*William Congreve,* The Mourning Bride

O f all the vice and violence, passion and perjury witnessed on the streets and in the homes of Lewiston during the town's first century, one story woefully epitomizes the twisted depths of depravity to which some people fell. A tale of wicked cunning, heartlessness and certain insanity, it is a fitting conclusion to this volume in the telling of Lewiston's history.

The urge to wreak vengeance warps the mind as few emotions can. Indignities and shame become excuses. Personal hatreds become justice. Jewell Freng succumbed to that disease. In her 2001 article "Reflections on the Desire for Revenge," Sandra Bloom provides some perspective:

> *People prone to experience overwhelming shame in response to disrespect are most likely to become angry, violent and retaliatory when shamed and may direct their anger at the person who has hurt them, at innocent others, or at themselves. Under the guise of a quest for justice, an ongoing desire for revenge may also serve as a defense against completing the tasks of mourning and thus impede therapeutic progress and improvement in life adjustment...An injured individual is rarely in the position of applying a balanced solution to a wrong that has been perpetrated against him or her.*

So it was with Margaret Hardy. Born in Missouri in 1842, Margaret came west, married and settled on the Palouse prairie near Moscow, Idaho. Described as "an old, scarred faced, beady-eyed woman," Margaret was familiar to local police courts, before which she had been arraigned for several minor offenses. Neighbors described her as "a woman not only of vile character, but possessed of an utterly uncontrollable temper."

In 1894, Margaret, her husband and their twelve-year-old son moved to Lewiston and lived in a house with an unnamed black prostitute. The living conditions compromised Mr. Hardy's fidelity, and Margaret soon learned that her husband's new friendship had benefits. Margaret was understandably incensed and, in her rage, began preparing to kill her husband. She would later say that he deserted her before she could get a good shot at him.

Margaret's mind began to focus on how to exact revenge on the prostitute who had tempted her husband. The woman had a two-year-old daughter, Henrietta, who was a mulatto child "but was nearly white." At the time, Henrietta was a ward of the city, which allowed no children to be kept in brothels, although, as we have seen in an earlier chapter, childcare was not unknown in bordellos. What better way to inflict pain upon the woman, Hardy thought, than to take her child?

Margaret approached city officials and posed a solution: the child needed a proper home, and she would provide it. The logic of her argument appealed to them. Margaret agreed to adopt Henrietta. In a process quite unlike today, the paperwork was completed within days, over the repeated protestations of the little girl's mother, who tried every means to block the adoption. The ease and speed of the affair raises troubling questions: was the child's white father still living in Lewiston? And if so, would not an adoption and relocation relieve him of possible embarrassment?

Margaret left Lewiston with her son and Henrietta, returning to Moscow, where she found a little shack near the city cemetery on old Troy Road (now Idaho State Highway 8). Her husband remained in Lewiston and returned to living with Henrietta's mother as her "male companion." It was the calm before a storm, "mere anarchy loosed upon the world."

In the days after Margaret's return, Moscow residents began to report hearing some disturbing talk from a woman who was, quite frankly, very disturbed. Observers later reported that Henrietta was treated badly and "was greatly afraid of the woman." Margaret began telling them that she was going to poison Henrietta and kill the child's mother, her husband and then herself. Neighbors protested and attempted to reason with her, but Margaret told them that she "had murder in her heart and must do it." On Sunday, February 10, 1895, she carried out the first step in her plan, and Henrietta died a horrible death.

Margaret's version of the event blamed Henrietta. She told investigators that she had prepared a dose of morphine for herself and was about to commit suicide when her attention was attracted by something happening outside her home. She put the morphine and a glass of carbolic acid on a low shelf and left for about forty-five minutes. By her account, Henrietta took the morphine and tipped over the glass of acid. Margaret said that she found the child writhing on the floor in unspeakable agony. The evidence at the scene created immediate doubts in the minds of the responding members of the Latah County Sheriff's Office.

Within days, they had established that Margaret adopted the child to punish Henrietta's mother and, failing to get rid of her, had poisoned her with the morphine and then, at the very least, applied the acid to the little girl. Henrietta's face and neck were terribly burned, with one eye nearly eaten away. Investigators could make out that the carbolic acid had been smeared on the child, but the infant had no acid on her hands. To the authorities, the acid was a ploy to hide the crime in the guise of an accident.

Carbolic acid was not an uncommon item in homes of the time, as it was used as an antiseptic. However, in full strength, it is highly caustic. Drinking carbolic acid to commit suicide was a very popular method in the late nineteenth century. Gertrude Jess tried it in 1923. Margaret's description of finding Henrietta rolling on the floor, convulsing, certainly pointed to the ingestion of carbolic acid. Doing so brings an agonizing death. The acid destroys the mucous membranes in the mouth, nose and the rest of the alimentary canal. The pain cannot be described. Carbolic acid paralyzes the heart as the victim gasps for air.

The county prosecutor envisioned another scenario: Margaret had administered a fatal dose of morphine. When Henrietta began to fall into a stupor, Margaret poured carbolic down her throat and smeared it on her face to create the impression that Henrietta had pulled the glass of acid over on herself. It was at best a circumstantial case. Henrietta could not speak for herself. She was only two years old. The county had buried her in the nearby cemetery without an autopsy.

The coroner's inquest produced immediate charges against Margaret, and she was jailed. Awaiting trial, she became "suddenly stark crazy." The sheriff's office viewed her actions with considerable skepticism. Some people claimed at the time of her arrest that she was of unsound mind. Observers were convinced that an insanity plea would be part of her defense, but they would be wrong.

Latah County Courthouse, circa 1890. *Courtesy of Special Collections and Archives, University of Idaho Library, PG5-1-11a.*

One might think that the indictment would have carried a charge of murder in the first degree, as her act was plainly premeditated. However, that did not happen. She was charged with murder in the second degree, which is defined as

> *a non-premeditated killing, resulting from an assault in which death of the victim was a distinct possibility. Second degree murder is different from first degree murder, which is a premeditated, intentional killing or results from a vicious crime such as arson, rape or armed robbery.*

First-degree murder was appropriate, but Margaret was a woman. In Idaho, first-degree murder carried a death sentence by hanging. No one was about to hang a woman. For that matter, there were no women in the state penitentiary among the more than one hundred inmates. The prosecutor did not want to give Margaret the chance to "plead her sex," an antiquated ploy to blame the weaknesses of women for her actions for being "the weaker vessel."

Margaret's day in court would have to wait. The Latah County Courthouse was the scene of a sensational incest trial, and a former city treasurer had just surrendered to the court on charges of embezzlement.

On the afternoon of March 5, Judge William Piper impaneled a jury. The prosecution spent that day and the next presenting their circumstantial case, resting on Wednesday afternoon. Her defense team of Charles Orland and George Goode, both Moscow attorneys, attacked the charge of poisoning, as no postmortem or chemical examination had been performed. They tried to convince the jury that Henrietta's death had resulted from her overturning the glass of carbolic acid on herself and not because of morphine. They rested their case on Thursday afternoon, and the jury retired to deliberate at 5:00 p.m. People noted that Margaret's sudden attacks of insanity disappeared as rapidly as they came. That would change the next day.

The jury met all during the night and returned a verdict of guilty of murder in the second degree the next morning. On hearing the verdict, Margaret went into a rage, swearing at the court, jury and her own attorneys "in unmeasured terms." Bailiffs forcibly removed her from the courtroom, and sentencing was scheduled for Tuesday, March 19.

Judge Piper confided that the bill of indictment had tied his hands and sentenced her to life in prison, the severest penalty he could administer. The audience, which had come to the courthouse to see how she would react, was disappointed when Margaret calmly received her sentence. Jury members would afterward tell reporters that a conviction would have been possible for first-degree murder.

John Campbell and the state prison, 1895. *Courtesy of the Idaho State Historical Society, AR42 #1241-B.*

Henrietta and her mother had gotten their justice, but would justice be served?

Margaret's transition to life at the Idaho State Penitentiary in Boise was problematic for the staff. No accommodations were dedicated for a woman. In the meantime, her attorneys filed an appeal with the Idaho Supreme Court on the grounds that on February 18, Piper had overruled a motion to bring the grand jurors into court, to be examined "as to their qualifications, both as a body and as individual members thereof." Her counsel contended that the grand jury had been prejudiced, speaking to outside parties not under oath. Some of the members had made up their minds about Margaret before they were even selected to weigh the evidence.

Several historians have debated the events of the next few months in Margaret's life. She was a mercurial prisoner. She would promise obedience to the prison staff and then fly off into violent fits of rage and screaming. She repeatedly attempted suicide, on one occasion by eating grass. Margaret's mental state was out of whack. She became known as "Mad Margaret Hardy." Was she already criminally insane when she arrived or did prison life push her from mental instability to a complete breakdown? The prison wanted some answers and quickly.

Dr. John Givens, circa 1904. *Courtesy of Idaho State Hospital South.*

On June 20, Dr. John Givens, the superintendent of the state insane asylum in Blackfoot, arrived to examine her. Prison officials briefed him, asserting that her insanity was feigned. Dr. Givens was joined at the penitentiary by Dr. Carol Sweet, a Boise physician, and another local doctor. The threesome was introduced to Margaret under assumed names. The *Salt Lake Tribune* reported, "She proceeded to go through a performance for their benefit, but they were unanimous in pronouncing her 'entirely' sane."

Armed with this professional opinion, prison warden John Campbell said that he would break her of her madness. She

Idaho State Insane Asylum, circa 1894. *Courtesy of Idaho State Hospital South.*

had driven the staff "to distraction, but he will conquer her if that is within the power of human ingenuity." Prison officials reacted with harsher treatment, fashioning a small, windowless cell in which she was kept in isolation. The method did not work. She set fire to the cell and would howl like a wolf for days at a time. Campbell finally gave up, saying she was "hopeless."

In October, the decision was announced that she would be moved to Blackfoot. Margaret had lasted seven months, one woman amid more than one hundred male criminals, isolated and abused. What sanity she had when she entered the prison had since left her. Given her propensity for violence, one can imagine the precautions that were taken on the railroad trip east to a vastly different standard of care.

In *Gendered Justice in the American West*, Anne Butler poses some relevant questions:

> *Within this story lies a strange tangle of logic. If Margaret Hardy was insane, why did officials act as if she were not? Did Idaho officials recognize that Hardy had always been mentally ill, and therefore their responses were harmful? Or did they decide that, since the prisoner refused to conform to penitentiary regulations, they would ship her to some other agency with more provisions for women? Or did they concede that their treatment exacerbated the instability that surrounded Margaret Hardy's crime in the first place?*

In late October 1895, the Idaho Supreme Court convened in Lewiston at the county courthouse (*Lost Lewiston* 18) and took up the question of Margaret's appeal but on November 20 ruled against her. The viewpoint of the court was clear concerning Margaret's mental state. Justice Joseph Huston wrote the opinion, in which he said, in part:

> *It is true, the evidence in the case is wholly circumstantial, but a careful examination of the record satisfies us that the circumstances proven, "taken as a whole and given them their reasonable and just weight, and no more, to a moral certainty exclude every other hypothesis except that of the guilt of the accused." The theory of accident put forth by the defense is entirely unsupported by the record. It is a mere suggestion of counsel...We think the evidence in this case left the jury but one of two conclusions: either the deceased, an infant under two years of age, committed suicide, or the defendant, possessed of a wicked and intractable temper, accentuated by vicious habits and an uncleanly life, in revenge of real or fancied injuries, took its life.*

Huston went on to make a surprising comment for a court decision, to which Justices Isaac Sullivan and John Morgan concurred:

> *If there is any error in the record, it is the verdict. Under the proofs, a conviction of murder in the first degree would have been warranted.*

Joseph Huston, 1899. *From* The Illustrated History of North Idaho.

Her sex need not have been an issue, the matter having been decided in a case the year before. Assertions were raised that new evidence had been discovered, but in Huston's words, "an examination of these affidavits fails to show any new fact." Case closed.

You might think that Margaret's story would lose its steam at that point, but subsequent events would prove people wrong. In April 1896, newspapers began reporting that petitions were being circulated in Moscow asking Governor William McConnell (*Hidden History* 85) to pardon her. Moscow? This was the same town whose residents had formed the grand jury and the trial jury, both of which were convinced of her guilt. This was the town in which Margaret had a rap sheet even before the murder. No pardon came. The June 1900 federal census lists her as an asylum inmate, one among scores of women incarcerated at the facility. Strangely, she is classified as "married." Whether she reconciled with her husband is unknown. Events happened so quickly in 1895 that the two may never have seen each other again after Margaret caught him in flagrante delicto.

On October 5, 1900, Dr. Givens delivered an address before the Idaho State Medical Society. Entitled "The Treatment of Common Mind Troubles," his comments provide us with a clear view of the treatment Margaret received. Physicians at the Idaho asylum firmly believed that to control the brain one must control the blood, as the brain utilizes fully 25 percent of the oxygen consumed by the body. It requires 20 percent of the carbohydrates we ingest to produce sugars that fuel the biochemistry in our heads.

Great care was given to proper nutrition for the inmates at the asylum. In his address, Givens recommended "good nourishing soups," in which the meats were well cooked. The properly baked breads would be a delight on any dinner table today. "The importance of fruits in the diet of the mentally sick is very great," he went on to say. "They are especially useful in the relief of constipation and in promoting glandular activity." Milk and milk products were not eaten with every meal.

Givens' comments concerning procedures for the skin are very enlightening if we are to understand the treatments Margaret received to calm her madness. He said:

> *The skin is the eliminating organ most directly, most easily and most safely under our control, and where there is evident imperfect depuration* [freeing from impurities] *of the blood the various forms of hot baths are of great service. One of the best of these is the hot water pack, made by wrapping the naked patient in hot wet blankets in bed and keeping him there from one-half to one hour, just before bedtime, with sips of cold water until free perspiration occurs for fifteen or twenty minutes, then rubbing him dry and putting him to bed for the night.*

Very light, easily digestible suppers were served, with no coffee, stimulating drinks or meats on the menu. The staff was very conscious that disturbed sleep undid the progress of the treatment. Well-managed exercise was designed according to a biblical axiom: "the sleep of the laboring man is sweet, whether he eat little or much."

It was only reasonable that when the state opened a mental hospital in Orofino, forty-five miles east of Lewiston, Givens was the man to build the new facility and put it on a proper footing. He selected a group of patients "whose insanity was of the mild type" and headed north by wagon. Margaret was not among them.

The confidentiality of state records shrouds Margaret's final years, even after 120 years, but evidence points to her death before the summer of 1910.

No evidence exists that she ever fully appreciated what she had done to Henrietta. It may well be that neither her incarceration in the state prison nor the time in the asylum undid the reality she had crafted for herself after finding her husband with a prostitute. It may well have been walking back into her home and finding Henrietta writhing on the floor, scared by carbolic acid and retching as it burned out her mouth, esophagus and stomach that was the tipping point. Only madness can block out that image. The violent and premeditated murder of an innocent child is a detestable madness.

Those who plot the destruction of others often fall themselves.
—Phaedrus

ON APRIL 1, 1930, CITY WATER department workers unearthed two graves at 113 Prospect Avenue, on the edge of Normal overlooking the confluence of the Snake and Clearwater Rivers. One of the graves held the remains of a "mature man," while the other contained the bones of a boy about ten years old. While officials thought the remains to be those of Nez Perce tribal members, none of the customary relics could be found. It is more likely that the graves were Chinese, as reports mention that the skulls had high cheekbones.

INDEX

INDEX

ABOUT THE AUTHOR

Wicked Lewiston is Steven Branting's fourth book published by The History Press about Idaho's most historically significant city. Since 2000, many of this country's leading history, geography and preservation organizations—including the American Association for State and Local History, The History Channel and the Society for American Archaeology—have honored Branting for the depth, scope and variety of his research and field work. In 2009, he was nominated for the American Historical Association's William Gilbert Award, which recognizes outstanding contributions to the teaching of history through the publication of journal articles.

The Idaho State Historical Society conferred on him the 2011 Esto Perpetua Award, its highest honor, citing his leadership in "some of the most significant preservation and interpretation projects undertaken in Idaho," whose governor awarded him that year's Outstanding Cultural Tourism

Award for showcasing Idaho's heritage. In 2013, the National Society of the Daughters of the American Revolution awarded Branting its coveted Historic Preservation Medal, the first to an Idahoan. In 2015, Lewis-Clark State College selected him for the Shinn Lifetime Achievement Award.